20 Winners at the Game of Life

Kaye Parker and Pat Watson

Order this book online at www.trafford.com
or email orders@trafford.com

Most Trafford titles are also available at major online book retailers.

Printed in the United States of America.

ISBN: 978-1-4251-5045-7 (sc)
ISBN: 978-1-4251-5046-4 (hc)
ISBN: 978-1-4251-5047-1 (e)

Trafford rev. 05/25/2011

 www.trafford.com

North America & international
toll-free: 1 888 232 4444 (USA & Canada)
phone: 250 383 6864 ♦ fax: 812 355 4082

FORWARD

THE HONOURABLE MYRA FREEMAN, OC, ONS, FORMER LIEUTENANT GOVERNOR OF NOVA SCOTIA

Twenty women, each at very different times in their lives, each from very different backgrounds and each headed in very different directions, share the one thing they have in common: the will to succeed.

Pat Watson and Kaye Parker have sought out twenty remarkable women to share with us their trials and triumphs, and in the telling, they remind us all of the power of positive thinking and the potential of every woman to define success in her own terms and to achieve success in her own way.

What makes 20 WINNERS AT THE GAME OF LIFE so inspiring is that its story-tellers are so much like us. They are the women you meet at the grocery store, at work or at school. Women you can relate to, feel for and want to cheer on. Twenty women, who, through their personal struggles and individual achievements, demonstrate the power and potential of every woman to find and feel fulfillment in small feats, as well as big accomplishments.

20 WINNERS AT THE GAME OF LIFE is a collection of real-life stories from real-life women of strength, character and courage. Insightful and inspiring, it is a book that will make you think about your own life and your own power to succeed.

Hon. Myra A. Freeman, ONS

Acknowledgements

In birthing this project, we would like to acknowledge the following loving and supportive people who continually influenced and encouraged us to create this collection of inspiring stories:

Our deepest appreciation goes to The Honourable Myra Freeman, O.N.S., B.A., B.Ed., D.Hum.L, LL.D, the first woman to be Lieutenant Governor of Nova Scotia and the first Jewish Lieutenant Governor in Canada. Special thanks for your supportive presence at several of our gatherings, and for writing the foreward to this book.

We also must acknowledge the incredible, dedicated and inspiring women who contributed their stories to this book. They continued to teach us as we worked together to make this project a reality.

We owe a debt of gratitude to Peggy Emberly who patiently helped us take this unwieldy document and hammer it into a workable manuscript. Your practical advice on electronic filing, chapter format and the time-consuming function of being the editorial board for this book is appreciated so very much. Without you we would still be trying to search for lost chapters.

Thanks to Mark Campbell, our senior editor, who had that important role of working with each woman individually, to help her find the right words, so that her message could be heard by readers everywhere. Your persistence and insights were invaluable, from the very beginning to the final stages of this book.

We also have to say thank you to our partners and families who remained supportive throughout what eventually proved to be a very long journey.

Thank you to David Watson, Pat's partner and true soulmate who continues to love, support and challenge her in wonderful ways. "When I think of David I think of how really extraordinary he is. I also want to thank John Howard, my incredible son, who has been an inspiration to me for 40 years."

Special thanks to Pat's mother, Alyce Roberts, who has always loved and supported her during her time on this earth. Thanks also go to Gayle Kato, Pam Lewis and Gilbert Roberts, Pat's sisters and brother who have encouraged her, challenged her, and supported her all of her life.

Thank you to Anne Fenety, Kaye's best friend, who was always willing to stop her own work to edit, offer advice or throw out a suggestion for consideration. Pat and Kaye made very few decisions without talking them through with Anne first. Kaye also would like to publicly acknowledge and thank her two daughters, Cathy and Deanna, and her late mother, Flossie Ritchie, who have been such positive influences in her life.

Finally, both Pat and Kaye want to acknowledge the many authors and teachers whose works have challenged and inspired them over the years.

CONTENTS

INTRODUCTION

This book was borne from the desire to empower women to tell their story. This is a collection of short stories from women in all walks of life. Success is not defined in terms of money or material possessions. Success is defined as a state of being; an inner feeling and knowing that you like the person that you've become.

We all know or have met women who, against all odds, have accomplished a great deal. This book is dedicated to all of the women who have gone before us who have fulfilled their lives but their story has not been heard. They have raised large families, taken huge risks and overcome many obstacles. They have been wives, parents, care givers, teachers, mechanics, scientists, cooks and decorators. They've worn a plethora of hats and still found the time and strength to do the things that they like most. The old expression, "Men build houses, women make homes" no longer holds true. Women can now do both.

CONTRIBUTORS:

Sue Bookchin, Principal – Skillful Means Coaching, Training and Organizational Development - Mahone Bay, Nova Scotia

Sue Borgersen, Visual Artist and Writer – Cherry Hill, Nova Scotia

Lea Brovedani, International Emotional Intelligence Expert and Speaker – Bedford, Nova Scotia

Faythe Buchanan, Speaker, Writer, Psychologist – Halifax, Nova Scotia

Dr. Jeanie Cockell, President – Jeanie Cockell Consulting Inc. – Tantallon, Nova Scotia

Ronda Degaust – Author, certified Neuro-Linguistic Programming trainer and Humanistic Neuro-Linguistic Psychology and certified personal coach – Halifax, Nova Scotia

Dawn Harwood-Jones, Partner – Pink Dog Productions and untv.ca – Halifax, Nova Scotia

Dawn Higgins, Owner/Operator – The Biscuit Eater Books and Cafe – Mahone Bay, Nova Scotia

Dr. Daurene Lewis, Principal – of the Nova Scotia Community College Campuses and sites – Halifax, Nova Scotia

Dr. Joan McArthur-Blair, President – Nova Scotia Community College. Joan lives in Tantallon, Nova Scotia

Debra Moore, CEO – Just Us Coffee – Grand Pre, Nova Scotia

Rev. Dianne Parker – Rector of St. Margaret of Scotland Anglican Church - Halifax Nova Scotia

Kaye Parker , President and Owner – Think PBBA Business Training, Dartmouth, Nova Scotia

Eileen Pease, President – Dynamic Learning Inc., Dartmouth, Nova Scotia

Dr. Pam Robertson, Writer, Speaker, Career and Life Success Consulting and Coaching – Halifax, Nova Scotia

Darlene Sanford, Owner – Nova Functional Assessments and Therapy Services in Lunenburg, Nova Scotia

Sharon Skaling, Speaker, Image Consultant, Personal Branding Expert – Bedford, Nova Scotia

Nancy Sparks, Race Relations, Cross Cultural Understanding and Human Rights Program Adviser – Halifax Regional School Board – Halifax, Nova Scotia

Michelle Strum, Owner – Halifax Backpackers and Alteregos Cafe and Catering – Halifax, Nova Scotia

Pat Watson, Singer – East LaHave, Nova Scotia

MORE LOVE...

SUE BOOKCHIN

> *I can hear our hearts crying... more love.*
> *If there's ever an answer,*
> *It's more love.*
> *~ Dixie Chicks*

I have discovered *more love* is essential for a successful life. Love creates the deep connection we yearn for as human beings. Love of the divine essence within each of us helps us find our way in this often-fractured world. And, perhaps, love in partnership with power constitutes true leadership. Love has been a chief informant on my quest of self-discovery, self-expression and desire to make my unique contribution for some common good. Three quotes taped to my computer screen remind me daily of my quest. They are touchstones for me in facing life's challenges and embracing what comes with grace and authenticity:

Send love to everything.
Give thanks in all circumstances.
Offer what you can.

The defining nature of my success thus far, is that I love my life. I live in a place I love (small-town Nova Scotia), with a person I love and admire (my husband, Derek), doing work that energizes, challenges and allows me to serve.

I feel embraced by a circle of family, friends, neighbours and colleagues that I cherish, and have artistic and spiritual pursuits that nourish me.

I have been lucky in having many opportunities to learn, discover and grow into the person I have wanted to become. I appreciate all my experiences, even the hard, scary or painful ones, and the deeply humbling ones that force me to confront my own misguided perceptions, self-righteous attitudes and erroneous assumptions. All prod me forward, urging ever-deeper acceptance and lessons in more love.

Family is the first purveyor of important lessons about relationships, acceptance and one's place in the world. I grew up in Brooklyn, New York. My parents provided a strong, safe container of family values. There were rules and chores, an expectation of high achievement in school, and weekend gatherings of extended family around kitchen tables with food and conversation. My dad worked multiple jobs, my Mom worked part-time, and I grew to appreciate the lessons in frugality and responsibility they conveyed. They helped me buy my first car and made me responsible for its upkeep and maintenance. They offered what they could toward university, and I paid back student loans for 15 years.

They even had me contributing to a retirement plan when I landed my first full-time job at 21.

Being scattered between New York, Nova Scotia and Los Angeles, I don't get to see my parents, who are approaching their 80s, my two siblings, or my little niece and nephew nearly enough. Our time together is precious, even more so as I age.

They are my kin. They have always been there for me. That never wavers.

When I was nine, I decided to become a nurse. It was one of those highly acceptable careers for girls who *wanted to help people.*

Interestingly, when my Dad was approaching forty and working as an orderly in a psychiatric hospital, he was offered an opportunity to return to school to become a nurse. Having dropped out of high school, this was quite a stretch, and his straight *A* transcript was quite an accomplishment. I guess I followed in his footsteps, which I thought was pretty cool.

Nursing was a whole different experience of *more love*. I attended my first births, deaths and lots of suffering in-between. My first job in a teaching hospital in the Bronx was a reality shock. So many demands, so little time for real connection. I didn't feel like I was making a difference. At 22 years old, I found what I was looking for as a Visiting Nurse in Westchester County, New York.

There were patients I visited at home three times a week for years. Some had crippling arthritis, rendering them bedbound, with few supports. Others had stubborn wounds that never healed. There was a young father who suffered a disabling stroke, and two young women, barely five years my senior, dying of ovarian cancer. I was so young, but somehow I was helping people through life-altering times.

I remember some of those patients vividly—their names, addresses, their fears and struggles, and the desperate needs of family caregivers for support, advocacy, and a shoulder to cry on. They relied on me, often as the only health professional they saw for months, knowing I would show up, do what I could, share a laugh that provided an all-too-brief respite from their desperate situations. Their experiences touched me deeply.

I became sensitized to the complexities of life with illness and dysfunction, and how people responded to that vulnerability and strain—some with incredible grace and optimism, others with deep anger, depression or self-pity. Given my inescapable conclusion that youth and vitality did not convey immunity to devastating illness or tragedy, I pondered how I might respond in similar circumstances.

As a middle child, feeling left out was a long-standing theme in my life. It sparked my earliest yearnings for love and inclusion. I lamented about never feeling as loved as my older sister or incurably cute younger brother. Given that history, I thought I tended toward being like the cranky, demanding patients I cared for—the whiners and self-pitying complainers who tried the patience of their loved ones even when their ailments were neither long-lasting nor life-threatening. That was a personal wake-up call I wasn't proud of.

Patients became my teachers. Like a courageous, good-natured man of seventy, a double amputee, who was determined to descend three flights of stairs from his apartment, on his rear end if necessary, to work in his garden. I marvelled at that kind of attitude.

I wanted to be like him—face adversity with grace and equanimity. I imagined there must be some quality of spirit, some intangible inner place or state of being that was necessary to cultivate that, and I had no idea how to access it until friends in New York introduced me to Kripalu, a centre for yoga and health in Lenox, Massachusetts. There, I learned more about love—self-love and self-acceptance.

How exciting it was to find a path for engaging and cultivating my spirit. I enrolled in a five-day meditation retreat. In the first three days of silence, I was frustrated with *not getting it*—whatever *it* was. On the fourth day, a guided meditation on self-love and self-care cracked open my heart to that little girl still inside me who always felt left out, unloved. Through a flood of tears, I discovered a core spiritual principle—it's always an inside job. Loving myself unconditionally was the remedy. If one can quell the ongoing monologue of judgments, of oneself and others, more love can enter.

I have lost count of the transformational programs I have participated in over the years. I am drawn to profound experiences of connection, of touching the sacred that connects us all, peeling away, like layers of an onion, the beliefs and patterns that no longer serve, deepening my well of strength, trust, self-love and courage.

Further on in my nursing career I discovered the relationship between love and true leadership while working as an assistant to the Vice President for Nursing at Manhattan's Mount Sinai Medical Center—the final leg of a Master's degree in Public Health.

Gail Kuhn Weissman was a visionary, smart, politically savvy and influential, creating some of the most innovative initiatives in nursing I have seen. She was also, it seemed, almost universally loved. Gifted at building relationships, even with so-called adversaries, Gail was masterful at making people feel cared about. Gail's associate, Pat Anvaripour, added another dimension of love in leadership—that of a patient, supportive mentor. Insightful and steady, Pat coached me without judgment, coaxing my emergent capabilities into being. There is simply no substitute for someone who can see and evoke the potential that eludes one's own recognition. As a coach, I try to *pay that forward* at every opportunity. Gail and Pat are two inspiring women, role models of a synergy between power and love—a standard I aspire to in developing my own authentic leadership presence.

The abridged version of what happened next goes like this: I came to Lunenburg, Nova Scotia for the first time to visit friends I met on vacation in the Caribbean. I loved it here. I fell in love with a man here. A year later, I finished my Master's degree, and, much to the chagrin of my family and friends, I picked up my roots from upper-east-side Manhattan and transplanted them in the unfamiliar ground of Corkum's Island. My lifestyle changed dramatically. I planted a hundred tulip bulbs and watched them be systematically devoured by rabbits and deer. I endured a season of getting stuck in snow and mud more times than I cared to count. I fulfilled a long-standing dream to learn stained glass, an artistic endeavour that continues to provide me with essential balance. In so many ways, Nova Scotia captured my soul.

The hoped—for long-term relationship ended soon after I arrived. It had been a major move. I knew very few people, was awaiting landed immigrant status, needed a place to live, had no support network and no source of income. I was shaky, feeling the loss, and very alone. That challenging time taught me more about love—love of the stranger.

I met a circle of women who noticed and welcomed me into their community. They were lifesavers and life supporters. They became dear friends. Among them were shamans, channelers, teachers and healers—a community of practice in healing and spiritual development, where I learned about the fundamental choice between love and fear. Now that's a lifelong practice.

Eventually I established permanent residency, became a Canadian citizen, and picked up my nursing career in unanticipated ways. Through an opportunity to lead a group of people in creating a vision for nursing with the Provincial Task Force on Nursing, I found my *right livelihood*. Invitations to facilitate group events, do strategic planning, leadership development and conflict resolution commenced. I trained, developed my skills and discovered a passion for learning. I have sought many learning opportunities since then, yet few compare to the Shambhala Institute's annual week long Authentic Leadership program in Halifax. In the eight years I have participated, it has enriched my work as a consultant, coach, facilitator and trainer, expanding my learning edge with global perspectives, innovative tools, and a stimulating learning community.

Nurse remains an integral part of who I am. While my work has expanded to include clients in business, government and non-profit sectors, I remain committed to giving back to the profession that was such a gift to my growth. In all, the principles are constant: nurture the best in people; enable healing and productive relationships; alter systems and structures to support people, innovative ideas and collaboration; and build community, connection, *more love...*

A journey to Nepal in 1991 rocked my worldview on love and deep acceptance. As a community of twelve able-bodied and disabled travelling companions, joined by four Nepalese high-school students and their teacher, we trekked in the foothills for two weeks. The journey opened me over and over. My first day in Kathmandu, I cried, overwhelmed by humanity in so many forms—the monks, beggars, merchants, children—and the visible reactions to our disabled friends. There is nothing like being in a place so different, you can scarcely imagine ever belonging to it, to confront one's own judgments, assumptions and fears.

I was humbled, challenged and enthralled as much with the people as the place. Amazingly, the people, with so little by western standards, were gentle, peaceful and happy to share their meager provisions. When I returned home, I stopped taking so much for granted. I stopped wasting water, realizing what a precious commodity it is on a global scale. I discovered my choices mattered as I internalized some invisible yet palpable correlation between the grace of my life and the material deprivation of others.

Gratitude, compassion and love expanded their territory in my being. Seventeen years later, I consider it a highlight in my life.

In 1993, five years after moving to Nova Scotia, I met the love of my life, Derek, across a pharmacy counter. I asked him out for a walk on Hirtle's Beach and the rest is history. Derek is a sensitive, endearing soul with a family history in Mahone Bay spanning ten generations. He brought his family into my life, a welcoming, uncommonly generous bunch, including two beautiful young daughters, Laura and Rebecca. Nothing I had done quite prepared me for being a stepmother. It turned out to be the most challenging and deeply humbling experience of my life. I was at a loss in dealing with teenage sensibilities, moods, habits, behaviours, and the sensitivities of a blended family. The girls became my most profound teachers in releasing judgments—more acceptance, more unconditional love.

We got through those early years, I think, through sheer perseverance on all our parts, and the reward since has been momentous. It is with a full heart and excited anticipation that I watch their lives unfold as independent adults, marvelling at the women of strength and character they are becoming. I am eternally grateful for these cherished daughters as we forge an abiding love and commitment for one another as chosen family.

My success continues to unfold as I engage my rightful place, honing the quality of my awareness and intention. It's like my garden—continual lessons in letting go and letting come. Every year, unexpected things sprout and some relied on things don't.

One must abandon even the illusion of control, working with what comes. I commit to ... *allow my living to open me, to make me less afraid, more accessible, to loosen my heart... (Dawna Markova).*

My work, family, communities, learning and teaching weave together continuously, alternately deeply challenging and immensely rewarding. All are opportunities to:

- *offer what I can*
- *give thanks in all circumstances,*
- *and send love to everything.*

~   ~   ~

SUE BOOKCHIN

While Sue was born, raised and educated in New York City, she discovered she's a country girl at heart, moving to rural Nova Scotia in 1988. She resides now in picturesque Mahone Bay with her husband Derek.

With a thirty year background in nursing and health care, Sue is principal of SKILLFUL MEANS Coaching, Training and Organizational Development. She feels privileged to serve through facilitating/hosting, training, leadership development, strategic planning, conflict mediation, team building, and coaching for personal and professional effectiveness; all in service to people, organizations and a world of greater sanity, connection, and peace.

Sue is also a stained glass artist, offering her unusual window hangings and jewelery creations around the Maritimes under the name Creations in Glass by Sueboo. For Sue, glass holds the opportunity to create, play, and manifest beauty, much like her pursuits in her impressive home gardens.

TAKING CHANCES

SUSAN BORGERSEN

There are many ways to become a failure;
never taking a chance is the most successful.
~ Anon.

I stand alone, centre stage at the Astor Theatre in Liverpool, wearing black trousers, white blouse and a red-spangled vest, the formal uniform of The South Shore Ukulele Players. A pink feather boa is draped around my neck. I have a neon red streak in my hair. My 1929 Martin ukulele is gently tucked under my arm.

A rivulet of perspiration trickles down my backbone. I look up. I am not an actor, merely the chair of a volunteer society that has just pulled off a feat many thought impossible: The First International Ukulele Ceilidh in Nova Scotia. The audience smiles. I know, before I begin my closing speech, the festival is a success. A success for Canada, the province, the town, the society, the volunteers. And a success for the lame dog of all instruments – the humble ukulele.

I take a deep breath, wave my ukulele in the air and, unscripted, open with, *Well - did we have ourselves a ceilidh or what?* The cheers are deafening. My speech is an attempt at witty.

I ramble about molecules on ukuleles, gush about the many ukelelians who have travelled to the tiny seaport of Liverpool from all points of the globe. People laugh. Am I that funny?

Don't they want me to wind up so that the "Hooley at the Ceilidh", the closing party, can get going?

And then it hits me. I actually did it. I had taken yet another chance. But this time I have a genuine feeling of personal success. I am sixty-something and my life has been quite a journey.

I grew up on the island of Cyprus. The eldest of five. An army brat. A life of sun, sand and soldiers? Not exactly. It was the 1950s and Cyprus was in political turmoil. My journey to the convent school, where I was a monthly boarder, involved intrepid drives through villages known for Eoka terrorists. Over the ten-foot convent walls, we frequently heard the chanting of *En-en-en-o-sis (Union with Greece)*, as demonstrators marched through the Nicosia city gates. As a flat-chested, snivelly 11 year-old, it was part of the daily routine, along with deportment, piano and embroidery classes. I made the move to a co-ed boarding school for military offspring two years later, where the distractions were as different as marmite to marmalade. Expulsions for promiscuity were the norm.

Boys were the main whisper topic at night, but for me, the late-developer (and flattest chest!) of the dorm, I could only listen and wonder.

I met my first husband in Cyprus. Terry was a British soldier and church organist. I was a Sunday school teacher. It stood to reason we would fall for each other.

But it was an unusual courtship, with Terry being posted back to the UK, leaving me with my parents and siblings for a further six months until the evacuation of British families in early 1964.

In England I slipped into the typical 1960s role for a young woman, beginning with marriage and two healthy children, Vicki and James, before my 23rd birthday. Success meant no hitches in the wedding plans, natural childbirths with no stitches, breast-feeding (from my now ample bosoms), and meat and two vegetables on the table each evening.

But money was an issue from the get-go. We begged and borrowed house deposits and furniture, re-painted the donated baby pram and had no social life. Friends were other young parents. After life on an idyllic Mediterranean island, despite its troubles, it was difficult adjusting to a grey damp England.

So we took a chance, gave up on struggling, and headed off to warmer climes. Like traditional wives through the ages, I became a camp follower.

On July 20th, 1969, the day man landed on the moon, we took our children to live in Bermuda where Terry landed the career break he strived for. Parties happened every weekend, and all weekend, keys-in-the-middle being the most popular sport. Our children, too, soon became little Bermudians and, to keep up with the financial pace (the material competition), I needed to work.

I have always had an enquiring mind and a fascination for solving problems. With the children quickly established in kindergarten, I tackled the problems of the Bermuda Credit Association. They needed to transfer manual accounts to computer. It was my *drop-me-in-the-deep-end* introduction to IT. I thrived on the challenge.

Things fell apart after a couple of years of living, what I felt was, a false, money-driven existence in a multi-layered Bermuda society. The tax-haven island was also going through political unrest at the time. A close friend was raped and murdered. It was my first wake-up call; our families had planned to return to the UK by banana boat together that summer.

Determined to do something for myself, I enrolled in a full time foundation course in art and design in England. It stood me in good stead then and now. In the mid 1970s, Terry landed yet another great job, uprooting us all once more.

This time to the island of Mauritius. Vicki and James attended a small French school in Curepipe, not far from the volcano.

The principal was an elderly, bed-ridden lady from Paris. Her philosophy on education was very open-minded. During one of our bedside chats, it emerged that she wanted her students to be *plus créateur, plus artistique.*

Madame cajoled me into teaching her French-speaking students how to draw and paint. I taught them to look, look again, and express themselves.

It was a delightful unpaid position, but to see these youngster's faces light up as they walked into art class, and glow even more when I told them that *this afternoon we are painting en plein air* was reward enough. That and the inspiration I drew from a woman who still pursued her life with such determination and joy in spite of declining health.

Back in the UK, in the early 1980s, serious career opportunities were opening up for women. Vicki and James were in good English boarding schools and Terry, now an expert in his field, was travelling the world achieving great things in the computer industry.

Me? I grabbed career opportunities with both hands and pursued a checkerboard of a working life, leaping over other candidates for great jobs. Climbing a precarious and prickly career ladder. Pitting wits against male counterparts on every rung. On one occasion, successfully taking my employer to a legal tribunal for a blatant infringement of equal pay. Not bad for one who had been a timid mouse in her formative years.

I topped the ladder as a Senior IT Strategy Consultant and Project Manager. I was a successful woman in a man's world. It was a lonely spot. It was also pretty desolate on the home front.

With a floundering marriage and the certainty that I had not spent nearly enough time with my, now adult, children, I was hit with redundancy. It was the late 1980s. Everything changed.

The economic slump in Europe had begun and I found myself on the career scrapheap before my 50th birthday.

Too old was the reaction to my numerous job applications. I questioned whether I had been successful at all. Was it worth the sacrifices? Especially the time missed with my children growing up? Would things have been different with the marriage if I'd remained a camp follower?

The solution stared me in the face: in all my successes, I had achieved other peoples' goals; never followed my own dreams. We had bought a summer home on Nova Scotia's south shore a few years earlier, mainly as a place to occasionally escape the rat race.

So I moved permanently to this retreat and started painting again. This was to be my pivotal point; my salvation; my way of taking control of my life. I also found the courage to accept the inevitable with Terry, and began divorce proceedings.

A serious asthma attack in 1992 put me in ICU. I had battled asthma since early childhood but was always determined it would never slow me down. Arne, then a friend and neighbour, was responsible for taking the swift action that saved my life. He helped open my eyes to what really counts: that it doesn't take heaps of money to lead a valuable life. We married in 1995.

Then, one day in 2003, the ukulele reared its little head.

I was having arthritis trouble with my finger joints and, in seeking a pleasurable way to exercise them, I signed up for *Ukulele for Beginners for the Over-Fifties*, a local evening class with a fabulous teacher. I was inspired. I caught the bug.

Internet contact with ukulele lovers in other countries revealed that uke festivals were going on around the world, each quite different and with varying levels of success. Ukulele enthusiasts flocked to them like moths to a flame. There was no such event in Canada. I had the seed of an idea.

This grew into a vision. It would be the First International Ukulele Ceilidh in Nova Scotia. If I didn't do it, someone else would. Through my involvement with local tourism, I was aware that, economically, the Province needed an event like this in Liverpool's shoulder season. I could see it. I could hear it.

It was no different than starting a company. At last, I had a new chance to use my years of business experience on my own terms, especially my project management skills. The first job was to establish a nonprofit society and get a competent board of directors together. Without these hardworking people, and their passion and belief in me, the festival would have never happened. They, along with our respective spouses/partners, gave overwhelming support.

On May 11th 2005, we were turned down for provincial funding and I dyed my hair shocking neon red. Why? I don't know. Maybe I needed a few minutes in the bathroom with a timer – something extraneous forcing me to isolate myself for 30 minutes while the dye took hold. That day, I understood that not everyone was prepared to take this chance. I concluded that success was not going to depend entirely on money.

It needed determination and the courage of convictions. It was about being passionate, positive, professional and tenacious.

It was about working hard. And most of all, it was about being happy.

But we did get our funding in the end. The ukulele ceilidh was a success – three days of concerts, workshops, jamming, parties, good times and making music with new-found friends. Over 700 workshop places were filled. Fabulous international, national and local performers took the stage. The 2005 festival laid the foundations for future ukulele ceilidhs in Nova Scotia.

I took a chance. With passion and conviction I persuaded others to take chances with me. The initial funding rejection was a mere rut in a bumpy journey. So I shouldn't give the impression that organizing a ukulele festival is a luau on an Hawaiian beach. Yet, it was also packed with happy times, boundless support and help that I will never forget.

Then something knocked me sideways. I received the province's Festivals and Events Volunteer of the Year Award. This time, much to everyone's relief, I really was speechless. The award belongs to all involved.

The success of the festival gave me confidence to take other chances—setting my own goals and accepting that I cannot achieve them alone. Like National Novel Writing Month 2006 and the International 3-day Novel Contest in 2007.

Solitary challenges I would not have contemplated without the knowledge that family and friends would support me throughout.

Walking deserted Cherry Hill beach with our dogs, I ask myself: in the grand scheme of things, do I make a difference? Probably not, but writing this has helped me understand that success is not necessarily about accountable achievements, it is also about experiencing and turning failure into something positive. It is about listening to those wake-up calls and seizing the day. It's about caring and being there for those you love, and to graciously accept the same in return.

It is also about taking chances with the humble ukulele and spreading a little unsophisticated joy.

~ ~ ~

SUSAN BORGERSEN

Susan Borgersen is a visual artist who writes. Her ambition is to be a writer who paints.

Until 1999 Susan wrote technical documentation, management reports, IT training manuals and secret poetry. In 1999 she took a creative writing course at the local community college and a monster was unleashed.

Today she writes 1000 words of fiction a day and her poetry is no longer a secret. She is also co-founder of Creative Holidays Nova Scotia, offering creative writing workshops and get-aways.

The remainder of her time is devoted to her very patient husband Arne, their restored (but forever-in-need-of-repair) Victorian home on Nova Scotia's south shore, their dogs, their gardens, her art (www.gloriousmud.net), and her 19 ukuleles.

LOVE AND PERSISTENCE

LEA BROVEDANI

Here are the three most important things I've learned in 54 years of living, my *pearls of wisdom* in case you're in a hurry:

- Love is the most powerful of all emotions.
- *A good head and a good heart are a formidable combination. (Nelson Mandela)*
- It's always best to buy good pantyhose.

I often hear people say they wouldn't change a thing about their lives, but I would. I would change the times I said words that hurt others, times I knew the right thing to do and didn't do it, and times I didn't sing when I had the chance. But I've learned from these mistakes. I've learned that saying "I'm sorry" is just as important as saying "I love you". I've learned that integrity isn't necessarily easy, but it always feels better in the end. And I've learned that success comes with taking chances and being willing to look foolish at times.

There is one thing I wouldn't change. I wouldn't change the people I've loved. I am blessed with a husband who still makes my heart beat faster, children who light up my world when they enter the room, and friends that inspire, guide and challenge me. And I have enough laughter in each day to give my belly a good workout!

Like many children, when I didn't like the rules of my parents, or was tired of sharing a room with my sister, I dreamt that I had been adopted, and that my true parents were a fabulously rich couple who wanted to spoil me rotten and give me everything

I wanted. Now that I am older, I know I wouldn't change a thing about the family I was born into. My parents married very young. I was born when my mother was only 23 – the youngest of five children! These were the days when wives and mothers exhausted themselves trying to live up to the standards popularized in *Father Knows Best* and *Ladies Home Journal*. Determined that no one would ever have reason to criticize her for having dirty, misbehaved children, my mother was always cleaning and disciplining.

When I turned one, my parents decided to move from the small farming community northwest of Edmonton where I was born, to the big city of Calgary. They managed to wrangle a mortgage for a tiny, 800-square-foot house. My father was a labourer – and a professional dreamer. He always had a new plan to make it big. He would talk about prospecting and finding the Lost Lemon gold mine, recovering millions buried in the mountains. From inventing beacons for downed aircraft to kits that converted canoes into catamarans, Dad always had a dream and a story. I've inherited my talent for theatrics and storytelling from him.

My mother was, and is, practical, hard working and disciplined. She was the anchor, making meals out of whatever was on hand, patching and remaking clothes so that we all kept up appearances. No one ever guessed how much our family struggled to make ends meet.

When I was eight, new neighbours moved in across the street – Marilyn and Wally Markwart. They were young, loved children and wanted to start their own family. At a time when I was going through an awkward phase, feeling ugly and unlovable, Marilyn loved me. She paid attention to me and became a surrogate mother. When my mother was too busy, Marilyn was there. She never told me to shut up, or that I talked too much. When I got hurt at school, teased on the playground, developed a crush on a boy, or got an A on my report card, Marilyn listened with love and empathy.

I was 12 years old when Marilyn finally became pregnant, but she didn't abandon me. I was with her the night she went into labour, walking up and down our street until she went to the hospital. I was waiting to see beautiful baby Darrin, when she came home, and I was the babysitter she would always trust. More than 20 years later, when I had my daughter, it was Marilyn who organized my baby shower.

Every person should have someone like Marilyn in their lives, someone who loves them unconditionally, listens to them without interruption, and sees something more in them than they can see themselves. It was Marilyn who taught me one of my pearls of wisdom—that love is the strongest emotion of all and accomplishes more than anger, shame or contempt in shaping a child's life. Sadly, Marilyn passed away on Mother's Day, yet not before I was able to tell her how much her love moulded me into the person that I am today.

When I was in my difficult teen years I rebelled against my parents rules and made many wrong choices. I spent a lot of time finding ways to skip classes. This resulted in my being expelled in Grade 12. When I found out the types of jobs available to me without an education, I went back for my diploma. Once I'd graduated, I found jobs that rewarded hard work and I moved up into management positions. I went from hating school to embracing life-long learning. I continually look for ways to increase my knowledge. I know that how we start out in life doesn't have to dictate how we end up.

I worked my way up in a small recruiting firm and went from the temp receptionist to the supervisor of a division. I was making a good living, but always loved a good bargain. That's how I ended up with pantyhose that were three for a dollar. On this particular day, I had a party to go to after work and had to pick up a few items on my way home.

When a hole appeared in the toe of the hose on the right foot, I didn't change. I took off my shoe and did what every woman knows how to do - pulled on the hose, twisted them into a little knot, tucked it between my toes and put my shoe back on. As I moved around the store, I could feel my big toe break through the hose on the other foot, so I repeated the pull, twist and tuck. When I got outside the store, I looked at my watch and began walking very quickly. I had been looking forward to this party all week and I still had to go home and change into something more appropriate. You see, there were two really cute guys that had been at a party the week before. They were gorgeous and had just started hanging out with our group of friends. All the women were vying for their attention and I had bought a special outfit that was guaranteed to get me noticed.

As I was daydreaming about them and hurrying down the street, I could feel the holes in my pantyhose getting bigger and bigger. My toes were no longer able to hold on to the shreds of nylon. Within sight of my car, both sides broke loose. I was now walking down the street with bare feet and shredded, baggy pantyhose bouncing up and down like Slinkies on a string around my ankles. I looked around for a place to go and remove the hose, but there was nothing—not a doorway, a tree, nothing but open spaces and parked cars. And then, I spotted them.

You guessed it – walking from the opposite direction towards me, less than a block away and approaching quickly, were the two gorgeous guys!

"Please, please, please God," I said to myself. *"Don't let them see me, have them be too deep in conversation to slow down. Have them miss me altogether."*

"Lea, Lea … is that you?"

I wanted to ignore them or say "no", but I didn't think that would work. With a face that was lit up like Rudolph's nose, I had a conversation that I have never remembered. When I went to the party, I avoided them, not knowing then what I know now—guys don't care about your ankles and being able to laugh at yourself will get you through any situation.

Despite such romantic setbacks, my career continued to blossom. The oil and gas industry was booming and when I was offered a job managing a personnel agency in Denver, Colorado that was involved in the industry, I jumped at the chance. I was ready to get as far away from Calgary as possible. A year later, a new political reality decimated the industry. Overnight I was out of a job. In July, I was the manager of a successful personnel agency in Denver, living in a 1,200 square foot condominium with a fireplace and all the amenities, driving a brand new sports car, wearing mink and living the high life. Yet by August I was back in Calgary, living in my brother's basement, looking for a job and wondering what happened.

In October of that same year I met and fell in love with Ric, the man I would eventually marry. Life can change so quickly. I learned that if you are willing to keep going and stay positive, things do turn out the way they are supposed to.

I followed Ric to Africa and we spent a year traveling through Kenya, Egypt, Greece, Yugoslavia, Italy, France, Great Britain and Scotland before eventually getting married in France and moving back to Calgary to start our life together.

I spent seven years as a full-time Mom and I loved it. My children are interesting, intelligent people, and fun to be with, so I never felt bored. When the children were a bit older and in school I went back to work and I quickly made my way back into management. Then, when my employer went out of business and I was left to begin again, I fell in love with an idea.

It started out with a book and the Christmas from hell. Daniel Goleman had written a book entitled "EQ, Why it Can Matter More Than IQ". It was on the bestseller list and I picked it up to read on the long flight from Halifax to California, where we were spending Christmas with my husband's family. It's what I was reading while watching my husband's brilliant, highly educated family argue and bicker and make choices based on feelings that created a highly charged, and very difficult, atmosphere.

By the end of the week I had witnessed what the lack of EQ can do to a family, and I started on a long learning journey, soaking up every book, article or website I could find on Emotional Intelligence. I went back to university and did my practicum on Emotional Intelligence for my Adult Learning Diploma. Understanding the simple concept of "choice in how you feel" allowed me to develop new relationships that were less inhibited and more meaningful.

In 2000, I went to a conference that changed the course of my life. The Nexus conference was held in San Francisco that year and world leaders in Emotional Intelligence were in attendance. The conference was put on by Six Seconds, the organization that Daniel Goleman studied when he was writing his book. I was determined to find a way to be part of this organization, I just didn't know how.

As Mandela said *"A good head and a good heart are a formidable combination."* Armed with this pearl of wisdom, I approached the director of Six Seconds and asked him if he would be willing to hold an international conference in Halifax, telling him I had a team of dedicated individuals willing to make the conference happen. I don't know what inspired me to believe others would be interested, but I felt so strongly that it was the right thing to do, I suspended disbelief and did what I tell my children to do when they really want something: "Throw it out to the universe."

When I had that conversation with Josh at Six Seconds in 2000, there was no one but me who wanted the conference in Halifax. Yet in a short period of time, amazing people who believed in the vision of bringing emotional intelligence to Halifax and with skill, talent and time showed up. In May 2003 the conference was held in Halifax and bringing together leaders in EI and human resources. People from all parts of the world attended and I was able to connect with others who believe that feelings are important, and that using the skills and tools of Emotional Intelligence makes the world a better place. Those skills have helped me to accept with dignity the pain of death and loss that life has since thrown my way, and the accolades and success with grace and deep appreciation.

Now I travel internationally doing what I love—bringing the knowledge and skills of emotional intelligence to a wide business audience. Good pantyhose, love and persistence has paid off!

~   ~   ~

LEA BROVEDANI

Lea Brovedani is a passionate and insightful speaker on improving leadership and personal performance using emotional intelligence.

She's been published in many business publications and is currently writing a book on "The Impact of Trust". Lea has spoken at a variety of organizations around the world ranging from Tourism Associations, the US and Canadian Military, financial institutions, and the health care sector.

She was asked to present at 4 international conferences on emotional intelligence to her peers. Her knowledge and application has garnered both friendships as well as respect amongst other emotional intelligence experts.

She lives her core values of compassionate honesty, integrity and excellence.

Wounds to Wisdom

Faythe Buchanan

*"It's not where you come from that determines your destiny;
It's what you do with the experiences you are given."*

Malcolm Buchanan was tall, pathologically thin, yet still handsome in a 1950's kind of way. His wife May measured in at 5 feet, one inch, and due to malnourishment was equally scrawny. This pair had met while working for a fundamentalist mission who allowed very little contact between the sexes, so they had committed to marriage without really getting to know their future life partner. Malcolm was a traveling evangelist in rural Nova Scotia. This meant that he and his soloist wife were living in abject poverty with their only source of income, the offering plates of equally poor families who came to hear the words of judgment delivered from the "pulpits" of little schoolhouses and community halls. The zealots' dwelling was a tent, with orange boxes for cupboards, and a hole in the ground for a toilet. The latter was perhaps my first physical hazard in life as while May (my mother) was carrying me, she was afraid that we would both fall in to this natural waste receptacle.

For further background to the matrix of my beginnings it might be noted that Malcolm was a war veteran from the Second World War. He had run away from home at age 17 and because of his height was believed to be older than his years and allowed to join the army.

His buddies had been blown up around him en route to action, and he was involved in D-Day and V-Day, thus had an incredible case of post traumatic stress disorder. While on the battlefield he had promised God that if he survived, he would serve said deity for the rest of his life, so he poured his angst into preaching to "save the souls" of those he believed were destined for an eternity in hell. At night he had nightmares as we heard from the loud moaning and disquiet he evidenced in his sleep. In the daytime he had rages whenever something triggered his feeling of being out of control. Malcolm had risen to a rank of sergeant in the army, so with both a wrathful God and the military training, he was a force to be reckoned with.

May, on the other hand, was used to poverty and abuse from her origins and lived to keep the peace with her unpredictable husband. Both secretly hoped they could "change" the other. Malcolm did not want children, however May did and out of this confusion of agendas, I was somehow conceived.

Upon learning of her pregnancy, May developed a hysterical paralysis, which was a precursor to her style of problem solving whenever life asked something of her which went beyond her comfort level. You might say that news of my existence was not exactly cause for celebration.

Welcome or not, I was born. In those first years which remain outside of my recall I am told we moved many times, living in back rooms of other people's houses, wherever the charity of the faithful would give us "a room in the inn" so to speak.

Sometimes those rooms would have broken windows, and the snow would come in at night. My mother tells me I was "not a smart baby," for I would sometimes take my mittens off at night leaving little fingers that turned blue with the cold.

Another feature of this gypsy life is that often my parents would leave me with whomever they could find to take care of a little person, for it was difficult to travel and do the preach and sing duo with a toddler. The record has it, that at age two (a time when a child needs consistency to figure out the world), I was staying with someone and had a child's version of "a nervous breakdown." In other words, I was seeing trains run over me, had a constant flow of diarrhea, and was basically psychotic.

To understand where parenting came in my parents' hierarchy of values, it seems that my current caregiver called Malcolm and May to tell them their child was in trouble and they needed to come and get her. Malcolm's response was that they were "doing the work of God and would return when they were finished." I guess I was in pretty bad shape by then.

Somehow the Universe was with me, even in early years, giving me an ability to be outside what was happening around me. My father had no idea that children do not know the system of cause and effect, so he began corporal punishment while I was still crawling.

I am told that at age three I looked out the window as my father was leaving for some divine mission, and said "I hope that man does not come back any more."

It seems that even as a very little person, I knew that circumstances were not defining me, they were something I did not like.

Life went on. I acquired a sister. Today she is my friend and a co-creator of our art and poetry book entitled *Remember Who You Are*. In early years I blocked her out. She was approved of by our father and the attention she received made it seem that she was important, and I was not, so for me she could not exist.

The physical and verbal abuse was constant for Malcolm had a hair-trigger rage response to anything he had not predicted or anything he did not approve of so there were many days when I wore welts from the leather strap which he saw as the instrument of my salvation. He veritably believed "spare the rod and spoil the child."

It was my privilege to attend many meetings in the above mentioned schoolhouses and community halls to hear my father deliver "hell fire and brimstone" lectures. During those speeches I was not allowed to move, and if as a five – six year old I would dare to show any interest in my surrounding, the public wrath from the "pulpit" was immediate. So I learned to sit very still. I had many hours of learning to *sit very still*. Could I have seen through a window into the future, I would have seen myself *sitting very still* and using this skill along with a very focused attention to hear the experiences of clients who sought therapeutic intervention to assist with resolving life's problems.

Very early on I became my own parent; at least, that is what happened inside my head.

At age seven I remember asking a visiting aunt and uncle if they would adopt me, as I did not think the family I was living in was a good place for me. Because they did not follow through with my request, I assumed that my parents had said "no". This left me with a feeling that we can't really choose who we live with, but we can continue to learn from what the Universe brings to us.

It might be said, that when it came to communication, Malcolm and May seemed to have nothing in common except their religious fervour. However, that was not the case. They both loved books, nature and music. And it was this latter talent that they agreed to sacrifice to help me develop. My mother tells me of taking me to the local piano teacher in Oxford, Nova Scotia (where we lived in a slightly more settled manner for six years.) The teacher indicated that she really had no more room for students and would only take me on if I would practice every day for at least half an hour, and only if I was musical. Upon testing me, her conclusion was "she's full of it" (music that is!), and at five years old I began a journey that has brought me many musical adventures, from festivals and recitals, many experiences as an accompanist, and hundreds of hours of relating to the instrument to express my feelings, compose, or just enjoy the beauty which is so available in note form.

There came a day when we moved, away from Nova Scotia, to Three Hills, Alberta. Another fundamentalist experience awaited us at Prairie Bible Institute. This is a place in the middle of the prairies where a town was completely divided.

The Institute had its own schools, store, generating plant etc., so the "separation from the world" would keep the beliefs touted from the "tabernacle" platform uncontaminated from the "world of sin," i.e. the people who lived "downtown." This was the era of the mini skirt, yet at PBI, the custom was to have a teacher standing at the top of the stairs, watching, to make sure none of the girls had their knees showing as the climbed to the upper floor. The Grade School was a place where my sister was strapped for not remembering how to repeat Psalm 23. I learned much about hypocrisy in this commune, for example the man who used to watch outside the massive church structure and inform my father if I missed a service, was also someone who was sexually molesting his own daughters.

At home, my father's rages and silences continued, as did the ever present conflict between him and my mother. Two more different styles of thinking would be hard to imagine—when she said white, he heard black, and so on through the rainbow of potential communication. I watched an endless parade of misunderstanding. Again, could the future have advised me, I would have seen thousands of hours worth of patient listening to couples and individuals who find communication, whether internal or external, to be a thing of mystery.

Teaching communication skills and compassion when perceptions are different had its birthplace in those childhood years.

The High School was co-ed, yet it was against the rules for boys and girls to speak to each other (in case they formed some kind of uncontrolled relationship).

I often forgot this rule, as to me boys were just another version of people, so there were copious detentions and calls home to my parents for my many thoughtless infractions.

Somewhere my strength was growing, and an unconscious desire to support those in pain was beginning to manifest. In elementary school I had noticed with some curiosity that although I was teased for being skinny, not popular with boys, pathetic at sports, academically unfocused, I would find other students telling me their problems—and of course I listened. The same thing was happening at home, to me, my mother would tell me her problems. Later she would tell my sister Joan. May was a very troubled soul who would share her marital woes with anyone who would listen, her favourite audience being her children. In those many hours of attending to my mother's complaints, although her behaviour was a betrayal of our relationship, I learned to step back and be an observer to those in distress.

In grade nine, I recall an incident where the teacher, a Mr. McLennan, dragged a boy across the front of the room by his hair. I was outraged, and stood up and told the teacher what I thought of his behaviour. He dismissed me from class with an order to go to the office—where I did not go, and there was no detention issued that day.

The beatings and demeaning behaviour continued at home. The atmosphere of Prairie Bible Institute was, for our family, very heavy.

Once again there was almost no income, but there was a food allowance and housing included in my father's position as teacher at the Bible School. I began to work for money as soon as I could. The music department at the Institute was superb. Because classical music and hymns were on the short list of what was not considered sinful, a great deal of energy and talent were focused on teaching and expressing music. My piano teacher kindly offered to supervise me teaching younger children piano lessons. These brought me a precious dollar per session. There was a system called "student work" at PBI where for 33 1/3 cents per hour we could work. I was occupied in sorting type for the print shop, sewing up large heavy paper garbage bags for use on the campus, filling communion cups with grape juice for the hundreds of meeting attendees, and peeling potatoes for the huge dining room.

My parents did not work for money—but so help me, I did. The ability to earn made the difference between treats (like a chocolate bar or a milkshake) or no treats. It meant learning to save to buy some clothes which were not hand-me-downs from cousins, or borrowed from my mother. It meant having a little efficacy in my own life. Once again – could I have looked forward through the lens of time I could have seen the time in my life where as a single parent with three small children (age one, three, and five when I left their alcoholic father) I had developed the motivation and stamina to work full time, finish University and fulfill my role as parent.

Without that early drive to earn what I could, to multi-task, I might have been a parent on assistance without a career, and insufficient mental and financial resources to fulfill my role as caregiver.

As in every life, the years unfolded. When I was 15, the family was transported to Edinburgh, Scotland. Yes, we moved from Three Hills, Alberta, to the capital of Scotland where everything we did or said was "just a wee bit wrong!" In a school where the masters wore "batman robes" and the fellow students, all in uniform, made fun of my sister and I for our accent and ways, I learned to adapt to differences.

With parents fighting at home, poverty reinstated by the lack of remuneration for my father's placement as head of a bible college, the teasing at school, and just not knowing how to cope with all of this, that is the only time in my life when I remember wanting to die. So this, too, brought me to a place of understanding that I would need later in life in my therapist's chair.

There are times when individuals view circumstances as too overwhelming to make life worth living. And then the Universe steps in to balance the sadness and bring resources to keep you going. At this low time, I turned to religion myself, as the only thing I could think of to bring meaning to my experience. I met some people who had fun, were friendly, and needed a pianist to assist in youth meetings.

From times of playing a pump organ in Crescent Beach to being accepted because I could play the piano for young people's meetings, I found a temporary solace in a Baptist church in Edinburgh. It would be quite some years before I would find that this too was but a place of learning.

Years later, in Sydney, Cape Breton I would move on from this religious refuge as I tried to "convert" a young man who asked me questions I had always put on hold. After weeks of soul searching I realized that religion had not brought me a grounding from which I could consciously live.

At the same time, the awareness of a Source beyond the human everyday awareness has stayed with me and contributed to a spiritual connection which is my birth right.

In Edinburgh I married a Scotsman, who three children later, turned out to be having a long term affair with alcohol. Thus, an introduction to addictions and a lifelong lesson in relating to the next generation.

I had finished Secondary School in Edinburgh. Then got a job in a typing pool at an insurance company, typing the same form, many times, every day. One day one of the girls said *Faythe, my room mate is doing something I think you would enjoy.* It was from that simple statement that I went for an interview for occupational therapy, got accepted and began my journey in learning and teaching life skills.

That journey has taken me through mental health clinics in hospitals in Cape Breton, Woodstock, Ottawa and Halifax. In each of those placements I have learned so much about the human condition, about what works and what does not. For the past 14 years I have been privileged to give service in private practice and to take and deliver copious trainings along the way.

Through all of these hours of listening, I have used my ability to sit still, my skill in being a respectful observer, the awareness that there is a Universe that is watching over us in a way we perhaps cannot comprehend. Now as a published author I have put my writings regarding the ultimate value which each of us can find if we take a moment to look inside, on paper for others to share. This written word is complimented so aptly by my sister's art work which resonates with the Spiritual sense of limitless potential.

From the times when my father would beat me, then lock me in a room to make sure I would not be comforted, I have come full circle to where I teach the art of compassion to our own souls. From the many places of transition and the hundreds of individuals who have honoured me with trust at the entrance to their souls, I can speak of the connection and mutual resource that we share as human beings.

It is with gratitude that I look back at a life experience that has trained me with understanding of the helplessness of trauma, the bleakness of poverty, the loneliness of neglect, the blindness of fanaticism, and the Love of the Universe that has helped me put it all together in an evolution of understanding and compassion.

~   ~   ~

FAYTHE BUCHANAN

*"There is no fear of failure
There is only fear of the unknown."*
~ F. Buchanan

Faythe Buchanan is an expert in "relaxing the subconscious" to help people unlearn the defences that make us think we are flawed.

In her personal and business consulting, writing, and speaking, Faythe delivers the message that there is nothing wrong with us; we have "just learned things that don't work."

Born in Nova Scotia, Faythe began her formal education in Edinburgh, Scotland, and completed a degree in occupational therapy from the University of Western Ontario. She has received training in PTSD, NLP, and Eriksonian hypnosis and has delivered numerous healing, instructional, and motivational workshops.

Faythe has worked in health care institutions, mental health units, for victim services, and community services, and has a busy private consulting practice. She has been listening to questions from the heart for 2½ decades and now has something to say.

Faythe is available as a professional speaker and has authored the book *Remember Who You Are*, reviewed by Dr. John DeMartini of "*The Secret*" fame.

LOVE IS ALL THAT MATTERS...

DR. JEANIE COCKELL

For Joan, my soul mate and for Mar, my daughter

My success is grounded in the love I have experienced in my life. I have experienced love in caring relationships with people, both personal and professional. I have also experienced it as passion for my work, and through continuous learning, growing, leading and contributing positively to the world around me. The title is a quote from my aunt, Jean Cornell Hooper, who inspired me with these words a year before she died. I have selected stories from the chronology of my life to illustrate my deepening understanding of love.

I was raised with much love in my family. It came with high expectations from my parents, especially my mother, who hoped I would go to university, travel the world, find a vocation, get married and have children. And so I did. My mother was a school teacher and instilled in me a love of learning. I did well in school and university, earning a Bachelor of Arts in mathematics. At university, I also explored romantic love and eventually fell in love with a man whom I later married.

After a year's teacher training, I went on to teach high school Mathematics. I looked barely old enough to be a teacher and would often be stopped by other teachers for running in the hallways.

I rode my bicycle or hitchhiked to school, wore long skirts, granny glasses with my long straight hair parted in the middle. It was the early 70s. I lived in sin with my boyfriend. I had very challenging classes of 35 kids, mostly boys full of beans and no interest in sitting at their desks. I fell in love with teaching. It was a way for me to make a positive difference in the world, in this case helping these teenagers uncover their mathematical skills.

After two years of teaching, I quit my job to pursue my love of learning through travel with my boyfriend to learn more about other cultures. We left our home in Vancouver for a three-year journey that started in Japan. Travelling through Asia, we stopped in Hong Kong for seven months to teach English. We committed to our own love by getting married there. Our travels continued through South East Asia, overland to Europe, across Europe and back home across Canada. It was very difficult at times, living cheaply in order to travel as far and wide as we could. Yet we learned so much about other ways of being—exploring foods, languages, histories, religions and other cultural practices.

This learning contributed to my deeper appreciation of love—my passion for respecting and celebrating differences among people.

Back home, I followed my passion for teaching, getting a job as a mathematics instructor at Vancouver Community College (VCC). This time, my students were adults taking high-school level mathematics to prepare for further education or to enhance their employment and life skills.

I loved seeing my students transform from having major fears about mathematics to being engaged and seeing themselves as mathematical beings. It was truly inspiring to see their self-esteem and joy of learning blossom.

Meanwhile, love grew in my family life when I became a mother. Being a parent has been one of my greatest experiences of love — unconditional love of my daughter and love of learning through all the challenges of parenting, especially the teenage years. Her dad chose to be a full-time stay-at-home dad. This allowed me to pursue my career more fully as opportunities for learning and growing arose.

One of these opportunities was being the mathematics department head. It was a great job; I spent half my time teaching and the other half leading the department.

I realized that I loved leading and sharing leadership with my team. Moreover, I found I excelled at building teams. I recognized team members' different strengths and provided opportunities for them to apply these. At the same time, I observed other leaders around me who were not so successful and became fascinated by what made leadership work, what inspired collaborative teams and what made people love working with each other even in their differences. My growing understanding of love and leadership led me back to university.

In my 40s, I completed a master's of arts as I continued teaching and leading.

I researched college women's concepts of power and leadership to more fully comprehend my own and to contribute to leadership theory. I found that, like me, the women in my study valued caring and connection as essential components of leadership. Leading by sharing power to make things happen was a key theme. It challenged the usual notion of power as control over others. Through my research, I developed a leadership model that expanded traditional skills to include caring and connection. Applying this model in my work strengthened my own leadership skills. My understanding of love, leadership and difference continued to evolve.

This evolution led me to a new area of passion and skill - speaking about my research.

I loved presenting and facilitating workshops, especially when people were inspired to look at their own leadership concepts and styles. At the same time, I continued examining my own leadership and my desire to make a positive difference in the world. I learned more about the impacts of difference, oppression and privilege. This led to opportunities to speak about the need for change around social inequities. Social justice and fairness for all people became essential to my idea of love.

After completing my master's, I became an Associate Dean at VCC. Once again, I had opportunities to learn by working with people from diverse backgrounds. In my team of department heads, I had two individuals who were deaf and one who was blind. This provided us with great learning about communication.

We verbalized voting so the blind department head would hear it and simultaneously raised hands so the deaf department heads would see it. I learned some American Sign Language and felt great joy in being able to communicate more fully, resulting in more caring work relationships. My understanding of love continued to broaden.

I led with passion, using my caring influence both within the college and provincially. Meanwhile, I continued to find fulfillment in teaching, facilitating workshops and occasional weekend courses. As I developed my facilitation skills, I became a trainer of facilitators. I regularly attended facilitator retreats, where we came together to learn collaboratively and creatively. It was at one of these retreats that I first heard of Appreciative Inquiry, a process for creating positive change, which later became a large part of my research and consulting. It was at these retreats that I fell in love.

As I was learning, growing and evolving my understanding of love in my professional life I was becoming very discontented at home with my marriage. We did not seem to share the same values in our lives. Eventually I realized the need to change as I was falling in love with a woman with whom I had facilitated for a number of years. We both decided to *blow up* our lives in order to create our future. It was the most difficult thing I have ever done, and the most significant to my success and to living a life full of love. My teenage daughter was not happy with my decision. Through patience and love, my new partner and I built a wonderful relationship with my daughter.

Those first few years were not easy, but my daughter developed into an independent, innovative, creative, hard-working and caring woman who continues to create her own amazing success.

My work continued to be full of passion for making a difference for student success. In 1998, I co-led a one-year project for the British Columbia Ministry of Advanced Education. We were successful in achieving our goals—to get the adult basic education programs of the school system and colleges to align so learners could get what they needed to achieve their work, education and life goals. At every stage, my desire to keep the learner as the focus of attention ensured that politically contentious issues were resolved amongst the competitive stakeholders.

This project led to similar projects and a decision to become a freelance consultant. I felt my desire to make a positive difference was constrained by the bureaucracy and by staying in one organization. I could have more influence from outside and with multiple organizations. I loved the freedom of working from home, doing contracts for a variety of clients. I was passionate about facilitating groups, helping them to work together better to achieve their goals.

To deepen my understanding of my facilitating practice, I completed a Doctorate in Educational Leadership in a group of twelve learners that included my partner. We became a very caring group of people, supporting each other throughout the learning process.

My research study with other consultants, *Making Magic: Facilitating Collaborative Processes*, strengthened my facilitating practice with resources and tools. It also enriched my perception of my work as a vocation, something I am called to do, my passion.

I loved the continuous learning and growing of my consulting work. For example, I took a contract consulting two days a week as the Dean of the Institute of Indigenous Government, a post-secondary institution focusing on First Nations students and perspectives. I learned so much from the students and staff about cultural differences and the history of oppression they faced, such as first-hand accounts of horrific abuse in residential schools. I realized how important love is in the healing process and in bridging cultural differences.

As I developed my consulting practice, I pursued my lifelong love of learning through continuous professional development. For example, I trained as an Appreciative Inquiry facilitator and trainer of facilitators, and began doing this work across North America. I learned to teach online, connecting people in different locations through collaborative learning via web-based discussion boards.

It was a challenge to learn how to facilitate in this mode because of the lack of visual and auditory signals, but my passion for learning overcame the challenges, especially because students so appreciated this opportunity. After completing our doctorates in 2005 we moved to Nova Scotia because my partner became President of Nova Scotia Community College.

It was a huge challenge to re-establish my consulting business across the other side of the country. I had to begin from ground zero to build a local client base and create networks. In the first few months, I lost my sense of self and success. I started consulting with people in career transition and found it helped me in my own transition. In coaching them, I reminded myself about the importance of connecting to people by appreciating and loving them and receiving their love and appreciation in return. Through appreciation and love, I soon regained my sense of self and success as I built my networks and consulting practice. I developed wonderful relationships and followed my passions through opportunities to learn, consult, speak, facilitate, write, and contribute to my new community.

My aunt was right. Love is all that matters to living a successful life. For me success has manifested through my love of people, learning, leading, consulting, teaching and facilitating. The experiences I have described represent some examples of how my understanding of love has evolved. Love is about appreciating people in all their differences and appreciating oneself in order to love and be loved. Throughout my life I have pursued challenges and opportunities to learn and grow, and to engage with what I love in my personal and professional life. Through this evolving understanding of love, I have strived to make a positive difference in my world, the outcome of loving well and following my passions. It has been and continues to be a most wonderful life full of love!

~ ~ ~

Dr. Jeanie Cockell

Dr. Jeanie Cockell, President, *Jeanie Cockell Consulting Inc.*, http://www.jeaniecockell.com, is a dynamic facilitator who is known for her creativity, sense of humour, sensitivity and ability to get diverse groups to work collaboratively together. She "makes magic," facilitating processes with clients for more appreciative living, leading and working together. "Magic" is the personal and group transformation to more authentic ways of being where appreciation is combined with critical reflection to enhance goal achievement and relationships.

Jeanie lives with her partner and puppy in the woods by a lake just outside Halifax, Nova Scotia.

CREATING YOUR OWN SUCCESS AS A WOMAN: THE STRUGGLE IS FINALLY OVER...

RONDA DEGAUST

Ask yourself the question, *"What is most important in my life?"*

What is your first response?

Does financial wealth come to mind or do words such as happiness, health, contentment, love and peace of mind have more resonance?

The words you think of are your values—the ways you measure your success.

Truly understanding the importance of living my life based on my own values has been an incredible journey filled with both pleasure and pain. For twenty years, I lived my life and based my self-worth on other people's values - what they wanted me to do for them. I was treated like Cinderella before she went to the ball; I was criticized for how I looked, acted and my ability—nothing was ever good enough. I tried harder to please, avoiding any actions that would be seen as wrong. I sacrificed my own values to gain acceptance from my mother and others. I repeated this pattern to overcome their obvious dissatisfaction with me; I thought it must have been my fault since strangers would also point out what was wrong with me.

Winning the approval of significant people in my life was my feeble attempt to find happiness. I never found it because I wasn't living up to my values—love, joy, contentment and, most importantly, peace of mind. Instead, I experienced considerable stress that affected my quality of life. It limited me in my career and prevented me from having healthy relationships or exploring hobbies that interested me, such as singing in a choir. It took time, but eventually I realized I would need to heal from this emotional pain and stress to reach the peace of mind that I was searching for.

If you are grappling with similar issues, or know someone who is, perhaps you understand the importance of changing such destructive patterns. In recognizing these patterns, you may conclude that continuing to feel this way has the potential be a major barrier to your success as a woman. I made the decision to take responsibility for my own success. I was determined to do what was necessary to overcome these issues by healing the pain inside. My healing started when I chose to take action.

Originally, I tried the traditional therapy route. When it proved unsuccessful, I decided to explore other options. Several people shared their experiences with NLP (Neuro-Linguistic Programming) and how it helped them make significant changes in their lives.

I knew from their stories it was what I needed. This process is based on changing unwanted feelings and behaviours. It's about modeling excellence and applying that excellence to whatever you want to achieve.

I felt these principles would help me start living a life filled with love, happiness, joy, contentment and peace of mind.

It was 1999 and, at that time, I didn't know of any NLP Coaches in Nova Scotia. I found one based in Pennsylvania who was willing to come here; however, I would have to pay all of her expenses and coaching fee. Determined to find my healing, I hired her. Her plan for me was a breakthrough session consisting of two half-days. It was a huge investment in myself on many levels, yet I was compelled to see it through; the pain was too great to bear any longer. I was confident deep inside that it would be well worth the cost.

I knew something amazing had happened to me that weekend during my coaching session. At the time, I wasn't able to precisely define the new feelings I felt inside. I experienced a newfound energy, and that felt exciting! I soon began doing things I had once only dreamed about. These dreams were for me alone—learning to sing being first on my list.

After several months of consistently feeling different and no longer responding to the criticism of others, I was convinced that NLP really did work.

It felt as if I had been released from a cage that, for years, held me prisoner inside myself. I became passionate about learning its processes and becoming a coach, helping people across Nova Scotia heal their lives and experience their own successes. I knew I would have to travel outside of the province to achieve my goal, and that this would not stop me.

Determined and motivated, I signed up for an NLP Practitioner certification course in the US.

Four months before my NLP certification course was due to start, I was diagnosed with a serious health issue (Melanoma, a deep skin cancer), scheduled for an operation and given a 50/50 chance of survival. It knocked the spunk out of me for a couple of days. Doom and gloom set in, and I didn't understand how this could be happening to me. I had lived such a healthy lifestyle, never smoking or drinking, paying strict attention to everything I put into my body, never lying in the sun, and now this.

Two days passed slowly, and then I made a decision that would change my life more than I could imagine at the time. I brazenly decided I was going to heal my body from this cancer before the operation. I had two months. I began by changing the way I was thinking and, with the help of my NLP coach, worked very hard to clear any negative emotions or thought processes that didn't support my healing. It was an incredible journey, and it ended with great success!

One week after my operation, the call came from the doctor's office. I was told the incredible news that I was "node free." This meant that the cancer had not spread to my lymph nodes and they had been successful in getting all of it. Of course I felt an immense sense of relief, yet I also felt disappointed. The disappointment was based on the statement, "They got all of the cancer." In my mind, this meant I hadn't healed my body before the operation.

I quickly brushed off this feeling and called my husband, Bob, to share the good news. Of course he was ecstatic.

A couple of weeks later, we went to my follow-up appointment with the surgeon. Out of curiosity, my husband asked how much cancer was in the chunk they removed from my leg. The doctor hesitated. He looked around the room before answering Bob's question: "Not a speck of cancer." A smile came across both our faces as Bob said, "You did it Ronda!" Of course the doctor didn't know what we were talking about. I'm quite sure he was relieved that we weren't upset about an operation that discovered no signs of cancer. My thoughts started to soar in many directions; the possibilities seemed limitless.

Still bandaged from my operation, I started my NLP Practitioner course in June of 2000 as scheduled and a new journey of understanding began. My passion for the things I wanted to accomplish grew stronger as my learning progressed.

My plan was in motion and I was making all the necessary changes to ensure my dream of becoming a coach came true.

A year later, I decided it was time to take my dream to a new level. I left my full-time job to pursue a career in coaching. Initially, I called myself a "success coach", yet this term didn't connect with what success meant to me, so I eventually changed it to "break-thru coach." I chose to specialize in emotional pain and stress relief by helping people change unwanted feelings and behaviours.

This felt comfortable inside my body and I knew it was right for me.

Through my journey and my work helping others, I've come to a realization about success. Each of us holds tightly to our own personal definition of it. To me, the true meaning of success comes from living what is really important to me in life. When you live your life based on your own values and connect to the motivating factors that make these values important, you decide the course your life will take.

Success holds only one meaning for me now.

It means *feeling good inside my home I call me.* I now base everything I do on whether it *feels right inside my body.* If I get an uncomfortable feeling inside when making decisions, I rethink things until they feel right! If opportunities come my way that don't fit with my values, I pass them on.

I know success is more to me than my financial statements and bottom line. Success is living my life in a way that holds true to what I believe in. What gives me satisfaction is becoming the person I was meant to be and living the life I was meant to live.

My experiential journey continues. I have achieved my certification as an International Trainer of NLP and, with my husband, have trained many NLP Practitioners from Nova Scotia, across Canada and from other countries.

I am also a published author of the first "NLP - Neuro Linguistic Personal Coaching Handbook," which is designed to help trained

NLP Practitioners & Master Practitioners coach their clients. What a joy it is to not only live your dream, but to also have the opportunity to share it and help others reach theirs.

Yes, I'm very successful in my chosen career since I'm doing what fits me—what feels good inside my body. This success is important to me because it also fits with my values of helping others. I help people using the skills I've developed through my training and experience over the years. My health has improved tenfold, as I no longer struggle with one issue after another, or the negative emotions of not feeling worthy. And yes, those old abusive relationships vanished from my life. The journey was long, yet worth it, and the learning I gained over the years I wouldn't trade.

I have also noticed a pattern through my experience and the work that I do: People struggle mainly from low self-esteem and put a high value on what they assume others think of them. Most of my clients struggle with issues of criticism from others, taking it as a reflection of who they are. The biggest life lesson I want to share with you is that people who criticize you do so to feel better about themselves and ultimately be a happier person because of it. Their criticism comes from a need to put others down to build themselves up. My heart goes out to these people since I know they have not yet reached a breakthrough point, and are still struggling with their own self-worth.

If I were to do it all over again, I would start my journey earlier. I would learn and understand sooner what feeling good inside my home I call me means to me. I would start living my life through my values sooner. Since it's impossible to roll back the clock, I am pleased to say that I have reached a true understanding of what it is to be a successful woman in many forms, including good health, strong relationships and doing what you love. When life challenges you, and it will, step back and view it objectively! Seize the opportunity for a positive learning experience from this challenge. It will enable you to grow to a level of success that you can only experience through your new level of understanding.

So many people who know my story, make the comment, "Ronda, you've come so far!" I always reply with a huge smile, "I hope this is not it!"

I would like to leave you with one of my favorite quotes by Dr. Milton Erickson: *"Until you are willing to be confused about what you already know, what you already know will never grow bigger, better or more useful. Continue to learn, continue to love and remember: your message is your life."*

~   ~   ~

RONDA DEGAUST

Ronda Degaust is an author, a certified trainer of Neuro-Linguistic Programming (NLP) and Humanistic Neuro-Linguistic Psychology, and a Certified Personal Coach.

Ronda specializes in emotional pain and stress relief and NLP certifications, helping people feel better on the inside so they can perform better on the outside. She accomplishes this by working with clients to eliminate negative emotions, improve focus, concentrate on life priorities and remove barriers to success. Through this process, Ronda successfully guides clients to achieving their life potential.

In addition to her love for helping people, Ronda loves singing, quilting, exercising and, of course, her husband and furry friends.

Eating the Clown

Dawn Harwood-Jones

It was the late 1970s. I was in Montréal because *Hank Williams: the Show He Never Gave*, a show I produced, was playing at the Lorelei. A country-music legend, Hank Williams died on the way to a New Year's Eve concert in 1952, and this very powerful play was a "what if". What if he made it to the "gig"?

The show is a moving piece of theatre; the audience watches the disintegration of a great artist as he counts down the hours to midnight, and to the end of his life. We avoided real theatres for this show; most of the venues we booked were the kind of seedy places Hank WOULD have played.

The director was passionate. So passionate, he dumped a customer's beer on the floor. After all, the waitress, who was not supposed to disrupt the mood, wouldn't stop serving during the heartbreaking second act, and that was in our contract! Right, our contract with, shall we say, the seedier type of *organization* that owns a few bars in Montréal. All of a sudden, two barrel-chested guys came up the stairs (both in three-piece pinstripe suits, and one of them wearing spats).

When one of them said, *"Get your director out of here now or we'll break both his arms,"* I thought *"If I survive this, I might one day think it's funny."* Not only did we survive, we toured Canada and the United States with this show to sell-out crowds and rave reviews.

The movie version of the play can still be seen on CMT. And I can now laugh about that incident.

G.K. Chesterton once observed that, *Humour is a rubber sword... You can make a point without drawing blood.* Music may have been my essential food group in life, but humour has always been my lifesaver. It saves us from drowning in the *now* and allows perspective. Is humour the key to my success? In some ways I would say no. The ability to move with the wind, to recognize talent when others see flawed humans, and the ability to respect people—those are probably the primary keys to my success, such as it is. Yet I do think humour saved me from many dire situations, and if I really look deeply, maybe it WAS an essential ingredient for success.

What is success? I'm not entirely sure, though many have told me that mine is a rich life—a life of success. My family of seven was poor but educated, and I lived a pretty privileged life, despite the need to count pennies. In fact it was idyllic until my brother died violently at the age of 25. It left a scar on my family, yet it gave us perspective on what was important and what was not.

All of us four remaining siblings, plus our two parents, set out to make sure we lived lives that we did not later regret. I dealt face to face with mortality by becoming a bit of a compulsive achiever. For example:

Artist
I was a professional portrait painter many years ago, while going to university and running a coffee house where some great folk musicians started their careers. I was honoured to have such talents as Bill Stevenson, Willie P. Bennett and Bruce Cockburn play my tiny bistro.

Producer
I have produced a lot of hit musicals. When producing *Hank Williams*, I partnered with Broadway's Lewis Allen and Mike Nichols—of *Annie* and *Who's Afraid of Virginia Woolf* fame.

This production also led to a partnership with country-music songwriter Roy Acuff. (What's more, I, who had hated country music up until this experience, danced with Roy in an elevator! Later I learned to respect Country music for its artistry just as much as I respected Jazz and "Serious" music.) This liaison with Lewis, Mike, Roy and with Nashville's kingpin Wesley Rose helped me understand how the real pros work.

After living in Toronto for a while, and promoting several great events (including the 75th Anniversary Arts Festival for Alberta, the Great China Circus in Ottawa and The Great Canadian Travelling Folk Festival and Good Time Medicine Show on the East Coast), I was seduced by Nova Scotia. The reasons were many: the quality of life I found, the honesty of the people who live here and, of course, my future husband. Soon after, I started an organization called Début Atlantic, a touring organization for Canada's top up-and-coming "classical" musicians. The organization is more than 25 years old now, and is considered a highly coveted "gig" for premier musicians from across the country.

In the early eighties I began working as a CBC TV producer and won several international awards for my productions, including two New York Film and Television Festival awards.

Even though CBC *outsourced* my department, I still love our public broadcaster and hope it survives some of those top bosses who have no sense of humour. My sense of humour helped me survive some rough situations during my 20 years at the CBC. It also made me laugh at the silly snobs in Toronto who, when they heard of my accomplishments, would say, *"What are you doing in Nova Scotia?"* as if to imply anyone of any worth should be in Toronto, of course (grin). They didn't realize I considered that I had moved up by leaving Toronto for the much more genuine quality-of-life province of Nova Scotia.

Real Success

And that brings me to the real meaning of success, at least as I understand it—Judy Parsons. I had been living in Chester, NS, for a few years and, although I missed my wonderful Toronto friends, I realized I did not miss Toronto. I couldn't articulate why the tiny village of Chester was so superior to Toronto until I personified it in Judy Parsons. Judy is Nova Scotian born and bred. I do not know anyone in Chester who does not love Judy. She is honoured by billionaires and fishers alike. Her equals are famous entrepreneurs and woodworkers. While this grandmother has a beautiful face, you will not likely see her on the cover of Elle, or even Chatelaine. (Although you should!) She is in her sixties, and is not exactly wealthy, famous or a runway model, but in Chester, she is adored. Why? Because she is more successful at being a human being than anyone else I know. She is good, fair, forthright and always a delight to be with. So that is the "Judy" factor. In Toronto, this amazing human would be invisible because her worth is common decency and humanity.

I want to stress that the wonderful friends I knew when I lived in Toronto were not that shallow, but the Toronto persona is… well, let me put it this way: success in Toronto is measured by fame, beauty and riches. And that is why moving from Toronto to the village of Chester was moving up in my eyes.

Nova Scotia

The other thing about Nova Scotia that contributed to my feeling of success is that you can be anything you want. I do not believe I would have realized my dreams in Toronto. The values and pressures were stifling. Here, I have hooked up with three great partners, Steve (Super Geek) Morrison, Ashley King, the brilliant British director, and writer extraordinaire Roberta Hancock (so extraordinary, I wish she could have written this). Together, we run Canada's first Internet television station—untv.ca and its sub-channel haligonia.ca—powered by many and diverse contributors. It's a place where hijab and nuns' veils can have intellectual comparison; a place where African Nova Scotian slam poets can blow the audience away during a taping of a show hosted by an activist Mi'kmaq comedian like Candy Palmater. untv.ca is the proud parent of a show that promises to become very popular on the old medium called television, *The Candy Show*. It's a show filled with humour, yet doesn't shy away from our most serious social issues; a show that actually lives and breathes diverse cultures and interests rather than doing it as an afterthought, or by checking boxes.

Candy and her show WILL be successful because she makes a point with humour and without drawing blood.

But no matter how big untv.ca and haligonia.ca become, I am just as proud that I am co-founder with Roberta Hancock of Pink Dog Productions. This is a video production company that produces "make a difference" videos for groups like The Mental Health Foundation of Nova Scotia, Elizabeth Fry Society, Health Canada and The Immigration Learning Centre. This company actually uses the powerful medium of video to change the way people think and act. Making a difference: isn't that what we all want to do?

Music

Music is my obsession and an essential food group. That is actually how I met Pat Watson. And it wasn't until I had lived in Nova Scotia for many years that I realized I was a musician. In Ottawa and Toronto, I took myself too seriously and was afraid of failure in music, so I never dared to perform or write. Now I conduct two choirs, sing with some a capella quartets and write musicals. The choirs I am part of may not be perfect, but we laugh during practice, and our audiences love us for the joy, passion and enthusiasm we bring to the music.

With friends and my partner, Malcolm Callaway, I have also co-created several musicals. Like my choirs, they are imperfect, but very popular, and again the packed audiences leave with some profound insights, even though they were laughing throughout the show. One of these musicals—*Death, the Musical (Karaoke at the Afterlife Bar and Grill)*—went from the tiny stage in Chester, to the main stage of Neptune, and then was translated into French for a run in Montréal. The CD of the show features some of the best musicians in Nova Scotia.

Another musical was featured in the Eastern Front Theatre's On the Waterfront festival. Actually, the first play I ever co-produced premiered at the National Arts Centre, so I guess I was spoiled by the instant success of so many of my musicals.

Family

Proud as I am of my many accomplishments, my greatest pride is my family. I am married to a most talented artist and writer, Malcolm Callaway, who has dedicated his life to making people laugh and think. And humour in the home was essential to our survival. I inherited a stepdaughter, Sarah, who wasn't so pleased with the situation. We complicated life further by adopting another girl, Stacy, when she was ten, and then took on a foster son some years later. A dog, cat, rat and two gerbils completed our family. Sure we had some pretty stressful times, like when my mother moved in because she had dementia. (The kids were TEENAGERS then - gaak!)

Yet, as my sister once pointed out, having teenagers in the house brings great stress but lots of laughter. I was not a very good parent, but luckily my daughters can laugh about my frailties. (Well, they can now.) It was during this time that we found out about Malcolm's cancer (he is clear now). To make matters worse, I was working under a highly abusive boss who daily tried to destroy all sense of self in all of my co-workers. That I survived this period is, to me, a success. I will never forget what my stepdaughter Sarah said, as she assessed the chaotic family life around her; *Someday this is going to be in a sitcom.* We all agreed it probably wouldn't make happen, because it was too far-fetched.

But it's a good example of how humour helped us survive.

What is Success?
So am I successful? Not as successful as Judy Parsons, but I have survived and, in doing so, have made some people smile. And success is waiting just over the next mountain.

That's my story and I'm sticking to it.

What have I learned that I offer as advice to you?

Dare to trust in yourself and in others. Who cares if you get burnt once in a while? That's better than not trusting anyone.

Dare to love. The only thing worse than a broken heart is never having anyone who might one day break your heart (be it child, friend or lover).

Don't try to explain yourself. It takes up too much energy and time. When do you see CEOs saying, "Well, I did this because…"? I learned that from my Broadway partners, Mike Nichols and Lewis Allen.

The deep end is safer to dive into than the shallow end (that's the phrase my business partner Roberta Hancock coined when we started Pink Dog Productions.) So if you think you're being thrown into the deep end, it's a good thing.

Be willing to lose your job to improve working conditions.

Be willing to wear blame that is not yours and to not blame others even when they are at fault.

Truth is harder than fiction to tell, but easier to stick by.

Live today like it is your last day, and treat your family like you will never see them again.

Get a grip! Is your life really that bad? Try living in a war-torn country. Or study a great artist like Srul Irving Glick. Although he experienced a concentration camp, Glick lived a life writing beautiful, positive music and encouraging love and forgiveness. Now that's an inspiration.

OK, those don't sound like terribly funny points of view, but here is my rationale: humour is the ability to take a step back and see just how funny our lives mostly are. My final thought on how to live a successful life is to get perspective. The kind of perspective that comes to you when resuscitating fish while entertaining Pierre Elliott Trudeau's family at a little circus. That's a perspective I'll save for next time (heh, heh), one that definitely requires a sense of humour.

~ ~ ~

DAWN HARWOOD-JONES

Until recently, Dawn Harwood-Jones was a television producer at CBC in Halifax.

One of the videos she produced while at CBC, called "Read to Me", placed in the finals at the 2004 New York Film and Television Festival. Dawn has also won several international awards for her promo production.

Dawn is now a partner in two vibrant companies; Pink Dog Productions and untv.ca. Pink Dog Productions produces "make a difference" videos and untv.ca is Canada's first Internet Television Stations. In her spare time, Dawn is a writer/producer of theatre (*Death, the Musical*, and *Fields of Crimson* for two).

Cycles of Life

Dawn Higgins

"Follow your bliss, find where it is & don't be afraid to follow it."
- Joseph Campbell

Following your bliss will never lead you astray. If you do what you enjoy, in your own way, with your own sensibilities, the worst that can happen is that you'll be happy. You'll also inspire others to honour their own unique paths.

I believe this is the definition of success. I also believe that what you imagine, you can manifest. Don't worry about how you will get there. In fact, dwelling on the details can impede the flow! Instead, feel the end result and let it unfold for you, in its own way. This means accepting the cycles of dormancy, germination, ripening, reaping and then letting go again. Now, in my mid forties, I can see these patterns, which I did not see, understand or trust in my youth. I created things unconsciously then; I was sometimes in the flow, sometimes not. It hadn't occurred to me that there may be a difference between the goals that society or ones culture may encourage, and the goals that an individual values.

During my twenties, I worked in the film industry of my hometown, Toronto.

I was following my bliss; I believed film was a way to bring my childhood passions for photography, music and writing together in one experience. I was particularly excited by experimental and documentary film. Yet after years as a starving student and many lectures about how nobody makes a living creating films about strange ideas, I built a career as a film editor working on productions intended for a mass audience. I worked six, sometimes seven days a week, made good money and had hardly any life outside of the industry. I became "logical", *practical and successful.* Other people saw me as financially successful and hardworking—traits my grandparents would have been proud of—but my work held little bliss.

Early in my career, I was invited to join a National Film Board program for young women filmmakers. Not even thinking about bliss, I chose to stay in television. Several years and meaningless, expensive, hierarchical, environmentally disastrous commercial productions later, I saw that moment for what it had been—a crossroads. Instead of documentary film, my passion, I chose commercial productions, which paid well. It was a choice based on fear, not love. I was fulfilling a very acceptable set of goals – they just were not my own. When The Oracle at Delphi advised one to, "know thyself" as the highest tenet, she knew what she was talking about.

A more authentic success came to me only after I decided to be more imaginative, more my own person. I took large leaps of faith and followed my own more intimate goals.

"Whatever you can do or dream you can, begin it.
Boldness has genius, power & magic in it. Begin it now."
~ Goethe

In 1992, my fiancé and I took a trip to Nova Scotia. We visited my brother, a talented boat builder and carpenter, now living in Halifax. For a few days, he chauffeured us around the province's magical South Shore. I found myself very attracted to the architecture, landscape and people. I also spent time at his workshop, located in an old building on the Halifax waterfront. The pier was abuzz with studios full of talented artists and craftspeople. I was amazed by the exciting and innovative work being produced, and even more so by the fact that I did not see this work in the local shops and galleries. Perhaps I could move to a small town in Nova Scotia, help sustain and grow a craft tradition and create a job for myself. Maybe a crazy idea, but it made me feel alive.

Back in Toronto, I told the head of post production of my plans. He said, "*Dawn, the only thing harder than getting in to film is getting out.*" He suggested I take a vacation. Most of the people around me thought I was insane. My fiancé was one of the few supporters I had. Within six months, we bought a house sight unseen and were living in Lunenburg, a town we'd only spent twenty minutes driving through. This was a leap of faith. I was moving toward something I believed in. Something I could imagine—not in the concrete details, but in the complete experience. I believed there was a great adventure waiting. I was following my bliss.

Once I started telling people what we were doing, all kinds of advice and information came my way.

Many told me about the great galleries and shops they'd found, and I would imagine them in my mind's eye, but the reality never matched my imagination. Eventually, I realized I could use these imaginary places as inspiration for my venture.

I held my vision of the perfect gallery in front of me. I used the richest, most vibrant colours, and kept focused on the mood that I was trying to invoke. It was like casting a spell. I wanted it to be inviting, joyful, unique and sophisticated.

We opened the following spring with one room of crafts, that, eventually, expanded into four. This business thrived in ways I could never have imagined. It supported my husband and I, plus many artists and craftspeople that became our friends. Working in the colorful, joyful space was a treat. I would often just stand there marveling at how this had all come about from a simple vision.

To thine own self be true.

What I discovered along the way was that my bliss lay in the creative, conceptual and start-up process. I got great satisfaction creating the concept and setting up everything from accounting systems to interior décor. I was not so energized by the more routine maintenance of running the business on a daily basis. Again I lacked the faith to recognize and follow this bliss. Seven years later we were ready for a new beginning and we sold the gallery.

The sale was shortly followed by the end of my marriage, and a long, introspective period in which I thought about who I was and what "success" might look like now. I needed to accept full responsibility for how I had lived my life and what I had allowed my priorities to be. The next four years were occasionally magical but, on a whole, extremely uncomfortable and challenging. I was single, living alone, had no work to obsess about, and uncertain of what to do next. I could not believe that I was still "adrift" after the first year, and began to despair of ever finding a passion to follow. There were moments where I felt things were "ripening," but most of the time I felt panicked and desperate.

It was getting harder to believe the answer was *out there.* I took a number of classes and did a lot of volunteer work.

Well into my third year of feeling my life would be forever on hold, a friend was raving about my biscuits over a pot of tea. I said, *Too bad no one will pay me to bake biscuits.* A door opened in my mind and I began to think about what I loved to do. I wrote down everything that was important to me, deciding to look inward for the answer. I thought about how someone might pay me to bake biscuits…

Henry Ford said something like "*it's a poor business that makes nothing but money.*" Money is essential, but there are many other, equally important, things worth working for. I decided to act from my highest intentions and to be "unrealistic", even "impractical." That felt good. I wanted to create something profitable, but it was also important to hire local women, pay them decent money, and engender self respect and autonomy.

I wanted to support our local food producers and promote ideas about seasonal and local food consumption. The business would be a boon to the community financially, spiritually, culturally and environmentally. It would come from my love of music, books and good food.

In 2004 I walked into a used book store and met my partner in love and life, Alden. I was working on a plan to begin my baking empire; he was looking to expand his shop. When we talked about our plans it seemed only natural to marry them together in a café/book shop.

At this time, we both had our houses on the market to raise capital for our new adventures. We didn't have two nickels to rub together, yet decided to start looking around for a location. Days passed into weeks, then into months. Neither house was sold.

The number of miracles that happened to make the opening of *The Biscuit Eater Books and Café* possible is truly fantastic. Perhaps the earliest and most important was finding our location. After a province-wide search and many promising prospects, we found a house/former restaurant off the beaten path in Mahone Bay. We were interested, but our houses had not sold and we had no money. On our second visit we met the owners and shared our ideas. We told them we were sorry we were in no position to make an offer. I remember feeling excited by the potential of the space, but helpless to move forward.

Friends were doubtful about the off-Main-Street site but I knew we could *build it and they would come.*

I could clearly imagine the colours. I could see my mother and me baking away, my friend Jo blending teas while Aiden sorted books and chatted with customers.

I saw the gardens in bloom during the summer and imagined customers curled up with hot chocolate on snowy winter days. We talked about having authors read and musicians play. We could have emerging local artist's display their work. It would be a real place of community.

This was our vision but we had no way ourselves to make it a reality. Either someone had to buy our houses or we'd have to win the lottery. Then, less than a week later, the solution came from somewhere entirely unexpected. The owner of the building walked into Alden's book shop and proposed we rent the space from him until both of our houses had sold—then we could buy his building. This solution allowed us to move ahead with our plans, but left him waiting before he could move on himself. It seemed unbelievable but there it was. (Later we learned he made that offer against the advice of his lawyer, his wife and his friends.) The day we closed the sale, he told us, *"I knew it would work. It felt good—the whole thing."*

Every morning at *The Biscuit Eater* I measure out the flour, butter and milk. I plunge my hands deep into the cool dough and I work all of the love and gratitude I feel into the biscuits. The oven is blowing hot behind me and I can see the day slowly unfolding outside the windows. I smell chocolate, fresh baking, coffee and spices.

Every day brings unimagined events, meetings and opportunities.

Daily I am surrounded by lots of laughter, friendship, community and love. Things here aren't exactly as I imagined, but they're so close it inspires awe.

I now have complete faith in this crazy process of creation which takes all kinds of movement and intention from both visible and invisible hands. Creating seems to be a kind of magic, of imagining and allowing, inviting and receiving. What I've learned is that it's not WHAT you do so much as HOW you do it.

Using your joy to guide you, it's an endless, unfolding, dance of energies that will sustain you for a time and then bury you until the next spring. Following your bliss will lead you down all kinds of weird and wonderful paths, and this journey is not without fear and pain. Success may be about accepting where you're at and redefining what your goals are. Creating success may be a matter of having the courage to say, "Yes" and making a leap at just the right moment—like catching a wave or a passing freight train. Who knows where it will take you; the bliss lies in the ride.

~   ~   ~

Dawn Higgins

Dawn Higgins lives in Mahone Bay, NS, where her love of (in alphabetical order)

Alden,
advocating,
baking,
book-keeping,
beauty,
great characters,
reading,
tea,
talking,
vacuuming
& writing,
have all come together in her latest adventure,
The Biscuit Eater Books & Café.

Leadership in Times of Change

Dr. Daurene E. Lewis, C.M.

Remember you are twice blessed,
you are black and you are a woman.
~ Rosemary Brown,
First Congress of Black Women, Toronto 1973

Atkinson School of Nursing, Toronto Western Hospital
The training of nurses remained fundamentally unchanged for decades. The combination of classroom theory reinforced by clinical practice had been successful preparing registered nurses to provide bedside nursing. I joined the teaching staff of the Atkinson School of Nursing as a Team Leader at a time when nursing education in Canada was being revamped. The training of registered nurses (RN) at that time was a three year hospital based program. Graduates of these programs provided bedside nursing care to patients in all hospital departments. Credentials licensing nurses to practice were obtained by passing a standardized written examination for the RN designation. There was a prescribed minimum hours of study and practice in various areas. The graduates had the knowledge and skill to work in all areas including speciality areas such as operating room, emergency room, intensive care unit, and recovery room.

This provided a nursing staff that could function in most hospital departments. Post graduate training was available for those wanting to specialize in a particular area.

Nurses in administrative roles were usually university prepared with baccalaureates as a minimum qualification.

It had been decided that all hospital based training schools in Canada would deliver two year programs. All registered nurses would require a baccalaureate degree in nursing as a minimum qualification to practice anywhere in Canada. RNs already practicing would be required to receive their degree in nursing by the year 2000. The plan also required that all hospital based nursing schools in Canada be phased out. In the interim nursing schools were to prepare nurses in two years instead of three.

The Atkinson School of Nursing was a 2 + 1 program. The first two years of training was comprised of an intense program of theory. The third and final year was an internship. During the internship year the students worked fulltime in the hospital. Throughout this time they experienced working all shifts. The students received a salary for the duration of the year equivalent to approximately ½ the salary of a fully qualified registered nurse.

As a faculty member I participated in discussions with consultants determining the future direction of nursing education in Canada that would include the phasing out of hospital based nurses training. In my role as team leader for the first year of the program I participated in development of a 2 year curriculum to replace the 2 + 1 program. Our team was also responsible to implement the shortened curriculum.

The challenges associated with revising and reducing a previously successful program were twofold.

Faculty would have to employ different delivery methods to compensate for the reduced clinical experience. The condensed program was designed to graduate nurses who would deliver basic bedside care. For example students in the two year program would observe a couple of cases in the operating room. In the

2 + 1 program the students had the role of scrub nurse. They were full participants in the surgical team and did not simply view a couple of cases from the observation gallery. As a result the graduate from the new program had some basic knowledge of the operating theatre, but lacked experience in the area. As a result they were not expected to work in the operating room after graduation without a post graduate course to qualify them. Graduates from the two year program did not have the knowledge or skill to work in all departments in a hospital.

My role as Team Leader was to assist the development of course outlines that facilitated teaching and learning that achieved many of the previous outcomes in less time. Managing change through this very dynamic chapter in nursing education and supporting staff was a major challenge so early in my professional career. Including staff in all dialogue allowed everyone to have input and reach consensus. As a result there was a sense of ownership to make the changes work.

Mayor, Town of Annapolis Royal
When I returned to Annapolis Royal from Toronto in the mid 1970s Annapolis Royal was undeveloped. There were several vacant storefronts on the main street with no apparent prospective tenants. I had just left my position teaching nursing in Toronto with a plan to learn how to weave from my mother and return to Toronto with her looms and yarns.

Before I returned home the superintendent of nurses at the local hospital called my mother with the days she wanted me to work. I therefore arrived home with a source of income to support exploration of the craft of weaving. I quickly discovered I had an aptitude to the craft and was promptly recognized in the Arts and Craft community. Three months after I started weaving fulltime I ranked either first or second in every category I entered in the Nova Scotia Designer Craftsman juried show.

My reputation brought me unsolicited business. This gave me the thought that perhaps I could make a living as a weaver. So I opened a business in the middle of the business district. I became involved in the Board of Trade and several tourist related organizations. At that time about 250,000 people visited the national historic sites in the town and surrounding area. Despite the number of visitors the town and surrounding area was devoid of services to retain them. There were a couple of motels and cabins for rent but no full restaurant. The visitors viewed the historic sites then sped out of town.

A federal funding program had assigned $6 million to the Annapolis Basin area. Most of the funding remained and the time limit of the agreement was expiring quickly.

The Board of Trade decided to spearhead an initiative to engage a consulting firm for a feasibility study on the viability of a number of infrastructure projects. A series of public meetings were held each one building on the previous gathering. Most of the meetings were facilitated sessions inviting input from those assembled. The final meeting, when the consultants presented their report, was in an auditorium that had standing room only.

The consultants commented that it was the first time they had been engaged in a project where participation increased as the study progressed. Usually many people are interested in the beginning. As the novelty wears off so does attendance. The enthusiasm generated from the feasibility study supported the formation of the Annapolis Royal Development Commission (ARDC). The ARDC hired an executive director to plan and implement a proposal that would access about $4 million of the federal provincial agreement.

The ARDC prioritized projects, secured funding, acquired properties and started design work. Regular update meetings were held with the community. A friend and I regularly attended these meetings and asked questions. We thought our questions were self evident since omissions and process were not always clear. We later found that a member of the Commission was being accused of leaking information to us so our queries would challenge the public statements being issued. The result was my friend was invited to join the Commission and I was invited to run for town council. In my first foray into politics I was successful in winning a seat on council.

There were a number of issues that I was now in the position to address. One that I had previously felt powerless to tackle was the provision of drinking water to the black community of Lequille.

Residents in the white community received water from the town reservoir/holding tank. Residents in the black community received their water from a plastic lined hole.

I volunteered to serve on the water and sewer committee and informed the black community that I was now in a position to help. Since the community was in Annapolis County and not in the town they decided to deal with the county and not the town. I then devoted my energies to the hospital board, mental health board and the heritage advisory committee.

In the next municipal election I was re-elected by acclamation. In Annapolis Royal each council elects its deputy mayor at the first meeting. My high school principal had just been elected to council and I considered he was the obvious candidate for deputy mayor. I was preparing to nominate him when nominations were called for. To my complete astonishment he nominated me. I was speechless. Since there were no other nominations the election concluded. I was still staring at him in disbelief. After the council meeting I approached him and asked why he had nominated me. I said "but you know me". His response was "that's why I nominated you". That public acknowledgement of my abilities and potential was pivotal in giving me the self confidence to show initiative and leadership.

During my time as deputy mayor my role filling in for the mayor increased. When the mayor's seat was vacated friends encouraged me to run for the office. My competition was a long serving councillor who was extremely active in all areas of the community. The by-election was held on December 22nd. Everyone expected a low voter turnout since people would be finishing their Christmas preparations.

I had visited everyone in the community and discussed what concerned them most. Just before Election Day I heard the comment that the town was too important to be represented by a black woman. I was very disappointed and prepared myself for failure. My weaving studio was directly across the street from Town Hall which served as the polling station. Many people came into my studio to wish me luck while others smiled and waved as they left the building.

When the votes were counted there had been over 80% voter turnout and I received nearly 85% of the vote. It was a stunning victory for me in a town where I had been born and raised, my father had been born and raised, as had my grandfather and great-grandfather before. When I learned the results I wept thinking of the weight on my shoulders. I had just been elected the first black woman mayor in Canada. We later found that I was the first in North America. If I failed as the first would any African Canadian coming after me be judged by my failure?

To be a good/effective leader you must respect your followers. Delegating authority, consulting your team and being prepared to accept responsibility for decisions. As a purely operational consideration I did not allow council meetings to last longer than two hours. That practice encouraged committees to have explored viable alternatives thoroughly before bring forward their motions to council. This was an extremely dynamic time in the town. The development projects had been completed and sustaining them became our challenge.

Since a small municipality like Annapolis Royal did not have the human resources to maintain a botanical garden, a live theatre, a boat haul-up and repair yard, a farmer's market and rental properties a strategy had to be implemented to ensure their continued success. It was truly amazing how the community came forward to accept ownership and responsibility for most of the finished projects. One volunteer group offered to accept their project even with the nearly $250,000 debt. I am very proud when I visit the town to see the projects thriving after twenty years.

This experience proved once again the depth of commitment a community has when they are part of the development and develop their own sustainability plan.

Closure of Bell Rd
I joined the Nova Scotia Community College (NSCC) in 2001 as principal of the second and third largest campuses in the College system. Each campus had nearly 1000 full time students and a separate administration. With part time, apprentices customized training students and continuing education the campuses served about 6000 students. The Institute of Technology Campus (ITC) on Leeds Street and the Halifax Campus on Bell Rd were campuses with very different histories and very different programs. The ITC had been built in the late 1960s as a technical institute. Programs included electronics, information technologies, machining and construction technologies. In the 1990s, trades programs from the Halifax campus were relocated to ITC. When NSSC was born in the late 1980s the campus also became corporate headquarters.

The Halifax Campus was opened in 1952 as a vocational school. By 2001 programs included business, adult learning, applied arts such as graphic design and photography. The only trades program at the Halifax Campus was welding. The structure was in a seriously dilapidated state for several reasons. Maintenance funds available in the operating budget were sufficient for routine repairs but were insufficient to fund infrastructure upgrades. Another contributing factor to the building's deferred maintenance was the College's desire to vacate the Halifax Campus and consolidate metro Halifax programs at another location.

In 2003 the province of Nova Scotia announced $123 million to fund infrastructure upgrades across the system, a purpose built campus in metro Halifax and the closure of the Halifax Campus and eventual closure of ITC. This was the largest single investment in education in the province's history. It signalled that Nova Scotians recognized NSCC as an option for post secondary education.

As principal my challenge was to close a campus with almost six decades of contribution to the education of Nova Scotians. It also was a landmark on the downtown Halifax landscape. We were to vacate the campus two years before the new campus was completed. Most programs are two years in duration therefore the temporary location would be the only experience a learner would have. ITC had a large proportion of male students; very few women staff, hence a very homogenous white male population. Halifax Campus had a large proportion of women both on staff and as learners.

Because of its downtown location it attracted a culturally and ethnically diverse population. The campus housed Department of Education's rehabilitation testing facility and deaf adult learning program. Ten percent of the campus population had a disability. It was not uncommon to have assist dogs and wheelchairs in the building for both students and staff.

Relocating programs from Halifax Campus to ITC would result in a major shift in demographics. I had participated in a number of changes over my career. I recognized that the reaction of all people involved needed to be addressed. Staff and learners vacating the Halifax campus would have very different needs from those having to accommodate newcomers. I was determined to make the transition as smooth and painless as possible.

The first step was to consult the experts. These included professional change managers and those who had successfully accomplished major cultural mergers. My management style and practice has always been consultative and inclusive. When people are involved in the process and have an opportunity to express themselves they are more amenable to accept change. This is based in the knowledge that change is threatening and therefore stressful. From previous experience I recognized that the stress of change must be managed to develop a successful transition strategy.

Two of the people I consulted had managed the merger of the Halifax Infirmary and Victoria Hospital into the QEII Health Sciences Centre. Neil Roberts was CEO during the merger.

Neil was extremely generous with his time and met with me on several occasions. He attended the first meeting with staff who volunteered to participate in developing a transition strategy. His counsel was invaluable in developing a transition plan. Gabrielle Morrison was also extremely helpful liberally sharing her experiences in the QEII merger. Both Neil and Gabrielle emphasized that there was never a too much communication with staff to keep them updated regarding progress.

I was aware that additional resources would be required. I approached my supervisor and asked for assistance. She recruited one of the deans and he assigned one of his staff to work with me 50% of his time. This individual was an architect and could make recommendations based on realistic assessments on space utilization. He produced floor plans that optimized space utilization. The Space Utilization Committee included all managers whose departments would be impacted by the move. This committee met regularly and provided input for me to formulate position papers which I prepared and submitted regularly.

The next step was to create working committees to address all areas of concern that were identified. Staff were asked their level of interest and many people volunteered. The first meeting of volunteers was a facilitated session on change management. This session identified the areas of greatest concern and also provided resources in change management support. Committees were formed to address the areas of concern.

The committees ranged from location of programs, communication strategy to plans for farewell to Halifax events. My greatest challenge during this phase was balancing the needs of staff and students and the College's appreciation of the confidence shown by the province in the construction of a flagship campus in metropolitan Halifax. My primary concern was for staff and students at both campuses and supporting and enhancing their ability to cope with the stress of transition. Showing respect, acknowledging and validating concerns required allowing everyone opportunities to look back and close the door before requiring everyone to look to the future and move forward.

It soon became evident that project management skills were essential for me to provide focussed leadership. To that end my assistant and I took a project management course. I also enrolled my assistant in a course in project management software. The course provided us with the skills to plan both moves, but also made us aware that external resources were also required. I engaged the services of our workshop facilitator to lead managers in a project definition exercise.

For two days seventeen representatives from human resources, maintenance, technical services, library, student services, faculty, academic services and internal communication developed the critical path to successfully vacate the Halifax Campus up until the move to the new campus was completed two years later.

A project management contract was designed and implemented. A project management team was created to ensure that timelines were being met. The team met every Monday morning at 0730. Information regarding progress was provided at the monthly campus meetings. If significant developments were made a report was sent to staff. Campus closing committees met in a parallel schedule. These committees focused on the closing of the campus. These committees included Fond Farewell, Open House, Mementos, and publicity. The Public Relations class took over the responsibility for the publicity. Timely internal communication was recognized as an essential element in any change management situation. In the absence of other resources I took the responsibility of communication with staff. Whenever I was made aware of issues I called a special meeting to address the concern. In the absence of facts people will speculate and speculation repeated by three people seems to magically become fact.

Final events making the closure of the Halifax Campus included an Open House where the community and alumni could tour the building. Presentations such as slide shows and other archival materials were available. Greeters and tours of the building were conducted by the Public Relations class. A variety of music performances were performed by harpists, singers and a men's choir.

A Fond Farewell evening was held for former staff. Former staff came from across Canada. One former staff member travelled from British Columbia, several people came from Quebec and Ontario.

The entire building was open with conversation areas throughout the building. The library with photos and other memorabilia attracted a great deal of conversation. The final event of the evening was a contest recalling significant dates and events. Time was taken to remember colleagues no longer with us. About 200 people attended the event. In one instance family of a deceased staff member participated in the evening.

Before staff started to vacate the building the union and administration hosted a farewell dinner. It was held in the former carpentry shop. The tables were draped in white linen and the caterer provided uniformed servers and bartenders. They also provided two chefs so that each person's steak or chicken was barbecued to their specification. We were serenaded by a group of staff who had written an Ode to the Campus. It was well received and a rousing send off.

When we cleaned out the walk in safe we found a supply of Halifax Campus watches. Each staff member who had been at the campus for 20 years or more was given a watch. To cap the celebration we had prepared a special gift for each person. A family member of a deceased staff member had given me a photograph of the campus. It appeared the photograph had been taken about 1952 shortly after the campus opened. The printing technology instructor had copies made which we had framed. The photos were personalized with each person's name. Staff were astounded and pleased that the effort had been made to commemorate their service. Staff appreciated the effort which they acknowledged by emails, notes and personal visits.

It was a fine balance to acknowledge staff's feeling of loss, but not embarrass the College by appearing ungrateful for the province's funding. However, I felt it very important to help manage staff's feelings of loss and separation. Most people would be working with new colleagues in new locations knowing that they would have to relocate again in another two years. The most poignant email I received said *Thank you for allowing us to grieve…we can now move forward.*

This was probably one of the greatest achievements of my career because it included so many elements. It was most gratifying for me when the fall semester started in September 2005. The population at the Institute of Technology had doubled, but there was no congestion or confusion. Staff commented that they had expected pandemonium and were pleased that registration day was seamless. Staff did not feel the stress and students noticed some changes, but no disorder. It was especially draining both physically and mentally for me. But the cooperation and support from my team to achieve success was well worth the effort.

It's better to burn out than rust out.

~ ~ ~

Dr. Daurene Lewis, C.M.

Dr. Daurene Lewis, C.M. is a seventh generation descendent of Black Loyalists who settled in Annapolis Royal in 1783.

In 1984 she was elected Mayor of Annapolis Royal becoming the first black mayor in Nova Scotia and the first black woman mayor in Canada. In 1988 she entered provincial politics and was the first black woman in Nova Scotia to run in a provincial election. In 2002 she received the Order of Canada. Daurene is a member of the Governor General's Order of Canada Advisory Council. The council reviews the nominations and advises the Governor General about recipients for the Order of Canada.

She is currently Principal of Institute of Technology Campus of the Nova Scotia Community College.

Free Fall

Joan McArthur-Blair

For Jeanie: love, laughter and magic
For Elly: sister, friend, protector
It is never too late to be who you might have been
~ George Elliot

I was flying, hands clinging tightly onto the rope, and then came the moment of letting go, feet outstretched and straining, and at last the landing solid and in one piece on the beam...I had done this many times, even though I was told not to swing in the barn. It was the coolest thing to do. I was young and unstoppable. The trick was to stand on one beam and swing out on the rope toward the other beam about fifteen feet away, until the rope started to swing back. That was the moment when I needed to let go and use the momentum to take me the last few yards. I had to land feet first and lean upright. I had all the room I needed, eight inches of narrow beam. The height of twenty feet or so from the barn floor never fazed me. I never missed, until one day and then I was in free fall. I can vividly remember the feeling— floating and plummeting at the same time, then blackout. My brother went to find my mom and told her, "Joan is dead." It became a family story, one retold at my brother's and my expense, sometimes embellished with details, sometimes lean and delivered as the punch line of other family stories.

I don't remember hitting the floor of the barn but I remember the free fall, that moment of feeling like you can float, yet knowing you are in deep trouble.

I think this moment defined me. There have been other influential moments in my life, but this one, where I did not die, opened in me a deep yearning to live life to the fullest. It inspired me to stretch, to understand the nature of being human and to maintain a sense of humour even in the dangerous times, because I know there will be a moment of free fall in the future when I will not escape.

It is this quest, this deep yearning and the passion for the possible that has defined my life, the person I am and the person I am evolving into. I want to share with you a few vignettes, poems and reflections. It is in these glances that I see myself peeking out from behind a moment that generated the possibility of becoming, of journeying forward to a place yet undefined and unknown. I believe that success, like leadership, is not a place arrived at. Rather, it is a practice of a lifetime, an approach to being, an ethos of capturing the accidental and the planned. I am currently a President and CEO, a success in the career sense; I am deeply loved and mentored by my partner, a success in my personal life; and deeply passionate about life at this moment, a success of mind. However, mostly I understand that success is this path I am on; the people I have met and will meet; the adventures that I have had and are still to come; and, most profoundly, the possibility of learning what it is to be a human being.

Success is merely a by product of an unstoppable longing to make a difference, to become one's vocation.

Leading in education has become my vocation and, as such, it has a powerful hold on me and I can neither turn away nor can I be different than I am as a leader. My leadership is driven by my passion for learning and the idea that education is at the core of building and sustaining a civil society. Parker Palmer, the powerfully reflective educator, writes about vocation as "something I can't not do, for reasons I'm unable to explain to anyone else and don't fully understand myself but are nonetheless compelling." For me, leading is like this; it is something I find myself compelled to do, without adequate words to describe why. Leading for me is a type of free fall full of possibility and of consequence. I intend to write more about vocation and leading, but I am distracted by a small vignette...

I am sitting here beside my partner; she, too, is writing about her success as a woman. I can hear the syncopated rhythms of our fingers as we type. I wonder what story she is telling about her life. It reminds me of times we have worked together, team teaching, facilitating—powerful women creating something we both believed in. I know her story will be more linear than mine. I often envy her organized mind. I imagine she is writing about love as I write about possibility. She has this way of arriving whilst I still journey and yet we are in tune, both working at things we love.

> *We travel, not knowing the way*
> *Pretending,*
> *the map detailed in our laps.*
> *We do not know what is coming*
> *nor where we go*
> *i do not want to travel laden*
> *i crave to travel light and quick*
> *i pack for conversation, make room for*
> *laughter, hope, and attempt to squeeze*
> *out despair*
> *i pack your gifts*
> *tissue wrapped and gentled*
> *I know I am unknowing*
> *and yet,*
> *I hold my map tight*
> *close in to my heart*
> *hoping to read in the dark*

Perhaps, for me, my vocation was born out of a love for language and learning. My mother taught me to read at a young age and it wasn't just the reading. She instilled in me a grand desire to explore the landscape of imagination through words. I can't remember how she did this, but I know it was in the early days before I went to school that I learned that words could transform. Perhaps this was my first success, a simple one, learning not just to read but understanding that reading was the basis of everything I would ever become, experience or imagine. It was her first great gift to me. She gave me many other gifts, amongst which, an understanding that women deserved an education, could be anything they wanted. She was a strong farmwoman who laboured hard.

She had been a teacher before marriage, forced to give it up when the school board told her that married women couldn't teach. Her story became my early understanding of the issues of equity, difference and power. Her stories and her experience shaped me and offered me insight in the future paths that might lie before me but always her greatest gift to me will be the wonder of words and the worlds that literature can create. Worlds that change and challenge us to our very core. I remember a time from when I was very young...

I am "up over the kitchen," a very cool place, not really an attic and not a finished room. It holds everything from an extra bed, to old hats and coats, but my favorite corner is a little shelf of orange crates that holds books from my Mom's years as a teacher, including the entire unabridged version of Grimm's Fairy Tales. I have read everything from Social Studies texts, English readers, to the classics, but today I open my friend Grimm's. I have a habit of opening it anywhere and beginning to read. Today it is the Brother and the Sister and their adventure in the forest. I go with them, hanging on every word knowing sadness is coming and unable to turn away.

I only have a little time with you so I am going to fast-forward from Grimm's to a Doctorate in Education. But first, there were adventures between youth and my late forties when I returned to school for my doctorate. Years of teaching; working in India and Pakistan; becoming a Department Head, Dean, Vice President— all stages of success. Perhaps the most profound personal journey was coming out as a lesbian in the early seventies before Ellen, and long before it was cool or acceptable. Being different coloured my successes in powerful ways. At the edges of my success was always the possibility of facing hate, of finding it right before me without warning. Being different has fuelled my drive to make a difference, to use my power and my privilege well. When I returned in my late forties to the University of British Columbia to undertake a Doctorate in Education, my goal was simple. I wanted to undertake research that would assist education leaders in understanding the nature of our work.

Talking Leadership, Talking Dirty

what if leadership talk was like sex talk
forbidden and secret
can you hear the conversation
the innuendo
slipping into someone's office
asking in whispered tones
"did you do it"
"was it good"
"was it good for them"
"are you going to see them again"
"you know I read about that position"
"what will your boss say if he/she finds out"
makes me want to talk leadership, you?

I conducted research on the Inner Life of Education Leaders. I was interested in what spiritually, ethically and emotionally guided them.

It was narrative research with the stories of leaders at the centre of the inquiry. At the core of leaders' inner lives was a trinity of inner life as social justice, inner life as sanctuary and inner life as moral framework. The leaders' stories were created into a play that brought to life the complexity and the influence of an inner life on leading and leadership. Becoming Dr. McArthur-Blair was one of the most powerful experiences of my life because of the success of attaining that standard of education but more importantly because of the opportunity to work with other leaders to explore the core of our work.

When I started out to undertake my Doctorate in Education I had no real intention of leaving my work as a Vice-President to become a President, but I was drawn by the college in Nova Scotia. Nova Scotia Community College was doing unique work as a portfolio college and it felt time to leave Vancouver for a new adventure. As I write this, I am President and CEO of NSCC and I love my work as a leader. The work of a CEO is a complex mix of education, politics, planning and academic endeavour. I have a grand passion for community college education and every time I meet a student whose life has been changed by the power of education it gives me courage. Education is the most powerful force in the world for freedom, civil society and social justice. I am honoured and humbled that I get to be part of something that changes everyone it touches. I get up every morning seeking new possibilities, new directions and new ways to be a leader so that those who work with me have the courage it takes to be educators.

I believe leadership is about deeply understanding hope and despair and being able to reside in those places of deep learning where hope and despair collide. It is in this place of collision that possibility resides and hope is generated anew.

Pondering Success

You invited me to write down my success

I wander through possible Latin origins, modern uses.
I revert to these places for safety
from
peeking at my life, peeling away skin and
bone, from looking at me.

Maybe success is like early history texts.
Part fiction, part fact.
And,
Only some wiser future generation will
Unravel which

I am standing above the jungle looking down. I am wearing a harness and have just clipped on to a zip line. I can feel my heart beating too fast and an inner voice shouts at me to get off this platform: "Nobody over fifty in their right mind would do this." I push off and begin to zip above the trees and I want it to go on forever, that feeling of free fall, of being at risk and invincible at the same time. I can see the catch platform looming up, and I know I need to brake, but I want just a little bit more, a few more minutes of being here above the world, of defying gravity.

It is over, my feet are firmly on the ground and my heart begins to slow. I look up and smile.

I know that success is fickle, just like free fall; one day my feet will not find solid ground. I grew up on a dairy farm and I saw the cycles of nature. I watched the crops go down in the pelting hail, yet no one suggested giving up and not planting the next spring. For me, this is the true power of success; it takes its own form no matter how much we plan. It wanders through its sister landscape of failure with surprising frequency and yet there are days that I get to zip across the jungle in wonderful free fall.

~ ~ ~

DR. JOAN MCARTHUR-BLAIR

Dr. Joan McArthur-Blair, Past President of the Nova Scotia Community College, is an educator with over 20 years experience in post-secondary education. She is a strong advocate for the unique work of community colleges and believes that access to education is the most powerful force for social good in our community. She has a special interest in leadership development and volunteers her time in the development of other leaders.

Sleeping with the Mosquito

Debra Moore

When I think about what success means to me, I think of an African proverb I once heard:

> *If you think you're too small to make a difference,*
> *try sleeping in a room with a mosquito.*

This proverb says to me that all of us can do something to effect change, and that someone doing a small thing can make an impression. I have never seen myself as doing anything big to change the world, but I see how little things I have done have had a major impact.

I am a child of the 60s and 70s, a time when the status quo was being questioned, and I wasn't any different. I have always had a passion for creating change whenever I saw things that weren't right. It could be anything—a recycling project, developing a respite program, coaching a girl's baseball team, getting involved in politics. I don't seem to ever do anything in a small way. In fact, I need be right in the thick of it.

Though my passion for change was shaped by the culture I grew up in, it was also profoundly influenced by my parents. My father was an accountant who moved our family from city to city as he scaled the public service ladder.

My mother stayed at home and looked after the family. I recall many heated discussions with my father, who was very strong in his opinions, over my burning desire to change the world, and I learned to live life depending on my own judgment.

It was during the last five months of his life that he and I found our way to each other. He realized, through his vulnerability, he only had to love me and not challenge me. His acceptance allowed me to continue to grow and challenge myself. At his funeral, my father's co-workers shared stories about him, how he had seen and nurtured their potential. They saw him as I saw him, as a mentor. I discovered something more: my father's idea of success was not necessarily tied to his position with the government, but the people he worked with. It's a lesson I've taken to heart.

My mother was my best friend. Whatever she did, in life or the community, she always ended up being the leader of the group. She also took every opportunity to show people how much she appreciated them, whether through thank you cards, words of encouragement, or helping out wherever she could. Most importantly, she understood that her three children were different and encouraged us to live up to our full potential.

At her funeral, many people talked about how much her acts of kindness had meant to them, and that she would be greatly missed. Her kindness continues to inspire me in how I live my life.

When I was 18, I took a summer job at a group home in Ottawa called Silver Spring Farm.

It was there that I met my husband, Jeff, an idealist who shared my passion for making the world a better place. We became best friends and discovered that we wanted the same things in life. Throughout our 32-year marriage we have worked together, using our complementary skills to accomplish our goals.

After completing Social Services training, Jeff and I made the decision to move to the Annapolis Valley, Nova Scotia, which we had fallen in love with during a previous visit. There was a movement at the time to phase out residential institutions in the region for people with physical and intellectual disabilities, and we became involved in the effort to find alternatives. Yet there was also debate about rebuilding the Mountainview home, known as the old County Poor House, in Waterville. We worked hard to make sure it didn't happen. Instead, Jeff and I were soon hired to head up a new initiative for the valley—a group home. We lived in this home for a few years until we had our first daughter, Sarah, and decided it was time to have a home of our own.

When we left, we invited two men with Down's syndrome to come and live with us. They had grown up in the Mountainvew home, had never experienced real family, and their needs were not being met in the group home. We didn't know then that this simple invitation was the start of something bigger—the creation of a L'Arche community in Wolfville.

L'Arche is an international organization that provides homes and work opportunities for people with disabilities. More importantly, the caregivers or assistants live with the people with special needs, forming a kind of family.

Jeff and I had visited several of these communities and had connections with L'Arche International. We knew from our experiences that we wanted to start one in Wolfville. In 1981, I approached Jean DeWolfe (the founder of the Flower Cart, a workshop for people with special needs) and Joanne Porter (then-Executive Director of The Flower Cart) with the idea. Their support and community connections helped make it happen. In fact, Jean came up with the community's name, Homefires. I became the executive director.

For a young person—I was 25—this was a lot of responsibility, yet my vision was clear. People with special needs belonged in our community. I saw beyond their handicaps and knew that, if we provided the right environment and integrated them into the communities of Wolfville and Greenwich, their gifts would shine for all to see.

We formed a board of directors, which became very important in my development as a leader. Jack Herbin, a third-generation jeweller, believed in me and patiently taught me all I needed to know about finances. Gi Forsyth and Carol Armstrong, community leaders, taught me a lot about working with people. Walter Murray, the minister at St. Andrew's United Church, taught me about tolerance, acceptance and forgiveness. I was gently moulded to lead Homefires.

As I was defining the kind of leader I was going to be, I harkened back to the examples my parents had set when as a child.

I wanted to be the type of leader that saw the potential in people, cared enough about them to speak the truth, appreciated their work and worked hard to exceed expectations. When I stepped down from the leadership in 1995, Homefires had grown to 50 people in five homes and was considered one of Canada's best community support programs. In 2006, my husband and I joined Homefires in celebrating 25 years. Over 500 people attended, and I noticed something profound.

They didn't see people with special needs as handicapped; they saw them as people they wanted to spend time with, people who loved them unconditionally, and people who created community around them. In that moment, I saw the success of our one simple act, how we had led the way for others to follow.

L'Arche had a profound impact on my family, particularly my daughters, Sarah and Susan. They've told me how thankful they are for the experience, and how it has made them what they are today. My relationship with these compassionate young women is something I treasure, and a real success in my life—the culmination of a lifelong dream to be a mother. Having children takes you out of yourself and provides many opportunities to learn. My children have taught me how to be humble, to listen and to forgive. I always say that I had Susan to keep Sarah company. As it worked out, in their adult years, they have become good friends.

My maternal instincts and passion for making a change led us to adopt Gregory in 1988. We first heard about him from the minister at the New Minas United Church. Gregory, who was a baby at the time, had Down's syndrome and was living in a foster home awaiting placement. I knew when I met him he was our little boy. The years that followed were somewhat scary. Gregory had a severe heart condition; yet the struggles we faced seemed to deepen our family ties.

Today, Gregory is the centre of our family. He starts each day with a smile and brings joy to everyone he meets. Gregory is also manager of his high school basketball team. After the team won a recent tournament, Gregory was called out onto the floor to receive the gold medal. When the announcer said, "this is a young man that represents true sportsmanship," the whole crowd came to its feet. I thought to myself that this young man, who was rejected at birth, is now valued for what he brings to his team and his sport.

Our passion for change, and our involvement with L'Arche has impacted Jeff's life and mine in a number of ways over the years—both personally and professionally. We had many opportunities to visit communities in third-world countries, where we encountered considerable poverty and injustice. We met many strong-willed people struggling to provide for themselves and their families—people with incredible dignity, a passion for life and a desire to be treated fairly. When we decided to leave Homefires, we knew we wanted to do something equally compelling with our lives—something that would allow us to make a difference in this world as we provided for our family. We found that opportunity in fair-trade coffee.

The seed for our business venture was planted in 1994, when Jeff visited his sister in Ethiopia. A maid, who worked for his sister, roasted green coffee each morning. Jeff, deciding it was the best he had tasted, came home with a 50-pound bag of beans and tips for brewing. Two years of planning and many great cups of coffee later, we formed a worker co-op with three friends and Just Us! Coffee Roasters Co-operative, Canada's first Fair Trade Roaster, was born.

We've had many challenges along the way, starting with our first order of coffee from Chiapas, made possible only when we put up our home for security. I discovered that I needed to build my business skills, so, in 2003, I enrolled in Management Development for Women, a highly intensive program offered jointly through St. Mary's University and Mount St. Vincent University. I enjoyed this program as much for what I learned as the women I learned with.

Challenges aside, our business has been a rewarding experience. I've realized my role has been to enter the lives of our third-world producers and help people to see their beauty and potential. During my time as CEO, I've tried to do business in a different way. A triple bottom line of people, planet, and profits. I wanted to be a leader that would give people opportunities, care enough to give honest feedback, and challenge our employees to do things that make our world a better place.

Sometimes, I couldn't meet people's expectations, and I was hurt as a result. When I am away from Just Us!, I hear that I am missed. Not so much for what I do but for my relationships with the employees, which is what I want to be valued for.

In the traditional business world, I probably would not have achieved great success. Yet, I did manage to lead our fair trade business into the annual list of Nova Scotia's top 100 companies. We've won many awards for our business and ethical practices. We've also been able to make a difference along the way, both in the lives of our suppliers, and through donations of over $500,000 to community-minded organizations.

So, am I successful? When I set out in my adult life, I wanted to make a difference, but the sad part is that, as Arlo Guthrie once said, *"Our world is in such a mess that it isn't that hard to do some good."*

So, my success turns out to be trying to be the best mosquito I can be.

~   ~   ~

DEBRA MOORE

Debra Moore has spent her life working with those people who have been marginalized in our society, first people with disabilities and then with peasant farmers in the third world. Her work with Just Us! has taken her to places she never imagined and to meet amazing people around the world working to change their fate. This has inspired and dramatically affected her professional and personal life.

May I Have This Dance?

Dianne Constance (Turner) Parker

God will rejoice over you with happy song ... God will dance with
shouts for you as on a day of festival.
~ Zephaniah 3:17

Waves danced along the shores of the sleeping cove, Ecum Secum, as a mother lay cradling her new born baby girl. A calm after the storm of child-birth fell over the modest home of Maude and Milton Turner. The rhythm of the baby's breath echoed the rhythm of the waves along the shoreline. Someone named God, who knit her together in her mother's womb, came close with twinkling eye and asked, "May I have this dance?" That night, November 10, 1946, God's new dance partner was given the name Dianne Constance by an attending friend and young midwife, Effie.

I love to dance; my very first memories are ones of my body moving freely to tunes played on the old gramophone or simply to rhythms within my own head. The Spirit of God dances among us, calls to us to appreciate and enjoy life and invites us to participate in the divine song that makes melody in the heart of all creation.

My ancestors had danced with Creator and Creation for decades along the shores of Nova Scotia. My heritage is German and English, and mother's family name was Meisner.

The Meisners came to Canada from Germany as part of the immigration influx in the 18th century and settled briefly at the Ovens and Meisner's Island on the south shore of Nova Scotia. Some members of her family migrated to the Eastern Shore. My father's roots were in England, and his ancestors immigrated to Canada in the 19th century also settling along the Eastern Shore of Nova Scotia. Hence the joining of the two families.

My childhood was spent in a loving, Christian home that centered around fishing, lumbering, church and community activities. Our daily lives were often filled with struggles as we were located in an area geographically rugged and economically poor. Like much of that community, our family of six people struggled financially. I found great comfort as a child in the stories about Jesus who was so loving and kind and considered the poor as important as the rich.

Some of my most memorable moments were spent at my grandparents' home, Franklyn and Bella Meisner, in Marie-Joseph. Family and neighbours gathered there on Sunday afternoons, singing around the pump organ, Granddaddy on the violin, Uncle Wilfred playing the mandolin, harmonica or accordion. We were allowed to sing only hymns or spiritual songs on Sundays. We would gather on Saturday evening if we wanted Granddaddy to swing into some fine toe-tapping reels. Even as a child, music and dance gave me energy and joy, bringing the zest of life to its highest peak.

Dance has always provided another mode of incorporating my spirituality, allowing me to express bodily the joy and pain of life, the giving and receiving of the sacredness of life. I danced through childhood, although not without falling out of step periodically. Childhood dreams and visions ebbed and flowed with many episodes of illness including a near-death experience at the age of 12 from appendicitis. There was no doctor nearby and certainly no money for transportation. After I was violently ill for three days, the dance almost ended. Finally, a family physician some 30 miles away came, spoke to my mother of very little time left, and promptly took me in his car to the hospital where he and two nurses saved my life. During my long recovery in 1958 and journey that same year through confirmation classes, I felt called to a vocation within the Anglican Church. I was all of 12 years old, and at the time, women priests were unheard of, in the Anglican Church in Canada.

Knowing within one's centre what one ought to embrace passionately in life was affirmed at my confirmation on September 11, 1958. Struggling with this sense of connectedness to God as choreographer of my future, I sought many hours in solitude floating quietly along the shoreline in a punt (a flat-bottomed boat) that my father had given to me as a gift.

Only two years later, I questioned for the first time the integrity of my dance partner when my father died just as I turned 14. I cried out as Job had, when he appeared tested by God.

Why did I not die when I came out of the womb? Why was I ever
laid on my mother's knees or put to suck at her breasts.
~ Job 3:11-12

Despite all the financial and personal challenges during that period of grief, I succeeded in re-entering the grace of the dance over and over again. When I graduated from Duncan MacMillan High School in 1965, it was still impossible to follow the "wee small voice" of God into Sacramental ministry because the Anglican Church remained closed to ordaining women. Therefore, I decided to enter the teaching profession with the intent to enter the mission field as a lay minister. I graduated from the Nova Scotia Teachers' College in Truro in 1967, a newly-licensed teacher with a job awaiting me in September at Harbour View Elementary School in Dartmouth. That deep sense of religious vocation surfaced continually while teaching. Troubled colleagues and others who were crying out for justice and hope in the dance of life were drawn to me to share their stories.

In the spring of 1967, just before graduating, I began dating a young man, Gordon Parker, who was also graduating from NSTC that year. Within a short time, I recognized that we moved to the same music of life values and dreams. On January 19, 1968, the night Gordon proposed, I hesitated to respond until I spoke clearly to him about how I loved him dearly but loved Jesus more, and therefore he might someday find himself married to a priest. I needed him to consider the effect that this might have on our relationship and on his career. His response constituted what I call a "holy moment", when he articulated that he was willing as I was to be open to God's will in our journey together.

I knew at that moment that God had provided me with a gift— an earthly dance partner. However, during the summer before Gordon's proposal, I traveled by train for the first time across our grand country and served on the Anglican Mission Van in northern Saskatchewan conducting vacation Bible Schools for children, officiating at services and compiling statistics for the Anglican Church. Returning to Nova Scotia, I began my teaching career, and Gordon and I began to plan our wedding. Twirling in the dance of love, we eventually married and successfully, within the rhythm of life, birthed two beautiful children, Donna-lee and Scott.

At this time, my life comprised nurturing our children, teaching, supporting Gordon as he completed his B.A., his B.Ed. and master's, ministering as a licensed lay minister and volunteering. While also establishing a private school in Liverpool and completing a B.A. and B.Ed. from Acadia, I moved from quiet waltzes to frantic jitterbug, to focused two-step, celebrative jive and other dance movements with God and others whom I encountered on my journey.

During those years, the underlying current of call to ordained ministry persisted in my thoughts and prayers. In 1976, women were finally allowed to be ordained in the Anglican Church. Bishops, clergy and lay persons continually encouraged me to embrace the journey to Sacramental ministry.

At the age of 42, I entered into the challenging, complex dance of formal discernment including studies to complete a Master's of Divinity at the Atlantic School of Theology.

I experienced some of the various feelings as if I were just asked to dance: hesitancy, self-consciousness, fear of doing something wrong, concern about being older than most of my dance mates, yet great joy and excitement at being asked, because I had long wanted to dance with this Partner to ordained ministry. I found myself trying to find the rhythm between the known of my past and the vast unknown of the future.

My past was people, a job, and a home that was a haven of security, and the future was people to minister to and live with, people I would need to learn to love and trust, a vocation that seemed almost unbelievably demanding of my talents and time and a home—I didn't even know where my home would be.

Why did I feel I must go through the door of accepting this call? Because God called me! All those years I had prayed that I could serve God in whatever I did. Now God opened a new door for this phase of my life, so I must go. It meant risking, sacrificing, leaving behind, but I knew I must continue the intimate dance with God. As a theological student, I traveled from Liverpool to Halifax, completing courses while Gordon and I raised our family, including caring for his mother Helen. Gordon, a geography specialist, taught in high school full time, was active as a scout leader and treasurer of Trinity parish church. All the while, I continued to minister in parishes as a postulant.

How did I manage? Because I believed: believed in God whose will is wholeness, believed in Christ who guided me on the journey, believed in the Holy Spirit who gave and continues to give me the power to do more than I can ask or imagine.

In the middle of such a journey, in the midst of the whirlwinds in which I found myself, where did I find a haven for a rest, reflection and relaxation? That haven came to me as faithful companions, women and men with whom I shared and listened to travel stories and the visions of our destination, in the caring and loving family relationships at home, and among people in the church community. As a result, I danced successfully through many courses, through my practice in ministry, through commutes in snowstorms, with a broken foot in a cast and among other related valleys and mountains. On St. Patrick's Day in 1994, I was priested with grand celebration by the Rt. Rev. Fred Hiltz in St. John's Anglican Church, Lunenburg. Since then, I have been present to many of God's people from womb to tomb in parish ministry including serving as Regional Dean and currently as Archdeacon of Chebucto Region (Halifax).

Although the priesthood continues to test and bless me beyond anything I could have asked or imagined, the most challenging part of my life's journey has been within the dance of grief. In 1995, during my first year as a parish priest, Gordon was diagnosed with prostate cancer and given 6 to 18 months to live. The cancer was very aggressive and began to consume his body and our lives. Grief for the both of us began at that point, his for having to give up so much and mine for knowing his earthly journey with me would soon end.

We often went to the ocean to sit quietly and become one with the ebb and flow of the waves upon the shore. Just like I had witnessed as a 12-year old child in Daddy's rowboat, we sensed part of the eternal and held each other in prayer. Gordon was rocked and cradled in the arms of God, as fragile as a seashell and as beautifully full of grace.

Prayer and medical science and an attitude of "living" with cancer resulted in nine more years for Gordon to be husband and soul mate to me, father to Donna-lee and Scott, grandfather to Zoe and Maggie, and mentor to so many more.

No matter how prepared I was as a professional for Gordon's death, my spirit was crushed when he took his last breath in the palliative care unit of the VG hospital on October 28, 2004; we had been married for 36 years. I expected myself, as a priest, to waltz through the grief but soon realized I, too, needed to sit in the depth of the pain - to literally abandon myself in the pain for healing to begin.

Like countless people I had counselled, I felt empty and alone even in the midst of a loving family, friends, parishioners and colleagues.

I knew that, *The Lord is near to the broken hearted, and saves the crushed spirit (Psalm 34:18),* but I had to intentionally sit in God's presence and walk through the darkest valley before moving fully into the rhythm of life once more.

In addition, I realized deep grief has no set timetable. One year after Gordon's death, I was diagnosed with cancer and found myself recovering from major surgery. It was in that forced period of inactive ministry and of quietness that I fully experienced the grief, now compounded with my own physical loss. And yet, with this gift of time away from full-time ministry and with the overwhelming support once again from family, friends, colleagues and parishioners, I found an oasis for rebirth and renewal.

You have turned my mourning into dancing, you have taken off my sack cloth and clothed me with joy .... Psalms 30:4-5.

The experience of such compounded grief has raised my credibility with those whom I minister in illness and on their pathway to death. God has continued to use me as a vehicle of compassion, offering strength, comfort, peace and hope to those who are suffering in pain, anxiety or in other areas of despair. It is in being present to others in the dance of life that one connects to a level of the soul where words cannot reach.

At this age of wisdom, I believe I see clearly what is most precious in my life. Dancing in the rhythm of life with Creator and creation is the secret of my success. Participating in this ever-present dance has led me to a strong sense of my own worth and value, and therefore to the worth and value of each human being. Dancing through life has drawn me into the deep mystery that lies at the heart of faith - that relationship between Creator and creation.

Most precious to me in succeeding is the assurance of the grace of God and its availability in the dance of life. To me this means that God loves me when I least deserve to be loved, that God accepts me - as I am, in so many ways unacceptable - that God forgives me again and again when I fall out of rhythm. That every new day I have a chance, a fresh start, to dance freely and to encourage others to embrace God in the dance of life to wholeness. God's grace frees me to dare to risk in the familiar and the unfamiliar. I have learned that if we dance intentionally with God, it doesn't matter where we dance; with someone so accomplished, we learn to trust the moves. Perhaps it is less important where we dance, than that the dance continue. And so I pray:

Flaming-Dancing Spirit come
Sweep me off my feet and
Continue to dance me through my days.
Surprise me with your rhythms;

Dare me to try new steps, explore
New partners and new partnerships.
Release me from old routines
To swing in abandoned joy and
Fearful adventure. And
In the intervals,
Rest me
In your still centre.
Amen

DIANNE PARKER

Dianne Parker is currently the Rector of St.Margaret of Scotland Anglican Church in Halifax, Nova Scotia and the Archdeacon of the Chebucto Region of the Diocese of Nova Scotia and Prince Edward Island.

She was born in Ecum Secum, Nova Scotia in 1946. She is a graduate of Nova Scotia Teachers' College, Acadia University and the Atlantic School of Theology. She taught public and private schools beginning in 1967.

She has a passion for life and enjoys sharing stories that inspire others to embrace life more fully.

Just Do It

Kaye Parker

Happiness is not in the mere possession of money.
It lies in the achievement, in the thrill of creative effort.
~ Franklin Roosevelt

As the eldest of five children, I got the undivided and adoring attention of my father, my mother and my grandparents for the first five years of my life. They encouraged me to try whatever it was I wanted to do. Perhaps this is why I grew up with the belief that I could do anything if I just tried hard enough.

My mother read to us every evening after the farm chores were done, but I wanted to read for myself. Whether it was a book from my father's childhood, the newspaper, or a cereal box, I tried to make sense of the words I saw, so I learned to read long before I went to school. One of my earliest memories of school was the mahogany bookcase that stood in the corner. It was full of books. By the time I left that one-room country school, I'd read every one of those books - some of them two or three times.

As a farm girl, I joined the local 4-H club. I was the only female, because this was a calf club, and most girls didn't want to lead a calf that was twice their size around a show ring. I found being the only female had its advantages. The boys automatically expected me to take the minutes, since I wrote better and more clearly than they did. That meant I was one of the officers of the club, which gave my confidence a boost.

Because 4-H sponsored speaking contests and travel to other clubs, and since I didn't know otherwise, I became very comfortable holding my own with the opposite sex in any debate or speaking contest or conversation.

I stayed with that 4-H club until I was an adult. My show calves won ribbons. I won judging competitions, and several trips, including one trip to the Royal Winter Fair in Toronto to compete nationally as New Brunswick's Dairy Princess. I didn't have to wear a bathing suit. I had to milk a cow!

School was entertaining too—from grade one right through to grade twelve. I loved learning, and talking, working and writing--even writing exams. I wasn't a scholar by any means. I just enjoyed the challenges school offered. I was editor of the school newspaper, and a member of the drama club, the debating club and the choir. When it came to sports, I wasn't very athletic but I didn't want to be left out, so I settled for being a cheerleader. Life was never dull.

Teaching was my only career choice. The fact that my parents couldn't afford to send me to university didn't give me a moment's pause. I'd held down a job through most of my high school years, and there were student loans available. Off I went to the city, with very little money in my pocket, and a strong belief that I'd make out just fine. I studied enough to get passing grades, fell in love several times, and eventually graduated.

After graduation, jobs were plentiful for teachers. My best friend and I took positions where we could share lodgings.

I had four grades in a one-room school, earning less than $2000 a year, and I've never been so rich. I was doing what I loved to do, and I was learning how to be a good teacher.

After several years teaching, I fell in love one more time, and married a terrific guy who knew exactly who he was, and who was quite willing to let me be me. We had two children together, both daughters, Cathy and Deanna. After Cathy was born, I decided I should go back to school. It was tough to raise a young child and find time to study but my husband never once complained.

Although I'd always loved school, I had not learned how to study. This time round, despite more responsibilities and less time, I was a much better student, because I had to be. Never a morning person, I learned to get up early, to study and do housework, before the sitter arrived. At the end of the day, the house was usually full of people - sometimes family, usually friends from university, who willingly pitched in to help prepare dinner, entertain Cathy, or help with an assignment.

After graduation, it was back to teaching. As the newest teacher at my junior high school, I had to prove myself. I was assigned a class of students, who while not exactly *difficult*, for a variety of reasons, from illness to a rocky home life, had challenges. Still, this was one of the most rewarding years of my teaching career. We got through the year, one small success at a time, and at the end of June the class presented me with the most magnificent bouquet of American Beauty roses I've ever seen. This was from a group of young teenagers that many had written off as doomed to fail.

After the birth of our second daughter, however, it was time to rethink my teaching career, and to re-invent my future. I decided to open a type of day care that suited my tastes: one for children who were either in kindergarten or primary school. I would offer the type of care I wanted for my own children…a home away from home, filled with love, good food, and activities that encouraged learning - with a little bit of fun thrown into the mix.

This day care lasted for more than five years, and I like to think I *helped raise* more than a dozen children. Most of the children who came that first fall stayed with me for the whole five years.

In addition to knowing they had a place to come to before and after school and at lunch time, I engineered games, visits to the skating rink and the sliding hill, the playground and, of course, the library. They are all men and women now, with children of their own, and I am proud to call many of them friends today.

Regretfully, it wasn't all fun and games. One of my charges was seriously injured in a car accident as he was crossing the street to my house. I will forever carry the image of that day in my mind and remember the ensuing weeks as he slowly mended. While I know consciously I could not have prevented his accident, there is a part of me that will always hold myself accountable.

These were also my volunteer years. I worked on a telephone help line, got a Headstart program for disadvantaged children up and running and sat on many committees in my church and my community. As I neared my fortieth birthday, I got restless feet again.

My first foray back into the adult world was as the manager of an employment agency. My main responsibilities were to find clients, find experienced workers, and find a way to match them up so everybody got what they wanted. Making those connections was very satisfying. I taught myself how to type and to write shorthand, so I would better understand the skills for which I was interviewing candidates. However, the agency wasn't as busy as I wanted it to be. I began to look for another position where the challenges were balanced by success.

I found that balance at Kings Landing Historical Settlement, just west of Fredericton. I spent ten years there and I sometimes think the Settlement and I matured together. I had opportunities I never dreamed I would have. I was hired as the Tour Coordinator, responsible for school visits. I soon moved into public relations and became the Director of Public Relations, in charge of all the marketing and promotion for the historical village.

My ability to stretch a dollar was invaluable as Kings Landing's marketing budget was small…and my dreams for the settlement were big. I believed then and I still do today, that museums have a responsibility to share their love of the past with everyone, not just colleagues in the museum community, and those who love history.

Admiring beautiful old furnishings, and watching people demonstrate how life used to be is a relatively passive experience.

By having each weekend of the season highlight some aspect of life in the 19th century, be it a *basket social* or a rifle shoot with the old muskets, more and more local people began to see Kings Landing as "theirs". Even the Winter Sundays, in the dead of winter, were well-attended. Our support locally was a growing group of Kings Landing "Subscribers", and we nurtured them with newsletters, dinners, and contests.

I travelled widely to promote the Settlement, speaking with people in the tourism community, the museum community and the travellers themselves. I wrote for and spoke to audiences in Canada and the United States, and was a regular on several radio and television stations. Out of this came an extra-curricular stint as a journalist for CBC radio, and a 30-minute program of interviews with well-known New Brunswick women, that lasted for two seasons on cable TV.

I was writing book reviews for the local newspaper, and a friend of mine asked me how the newspaper had happened to choose me to write their book reviews. I told him the newspaper editors hadn't chosen me. I'd asked them to let me write those reviews. I felt I was creating a niche that was perfect for me. I was evolving.

Then, early in 1987, my wonderful world was turned on its end. Within the space of seventeen days, first my father-in-law, then my father and then my husband died. My husband suffered a massive heart attack just hours after we returned home from my father's funeral. Within minutes he too was dead. My father-in-law had been in hospital, so while his death was sudden, it wasn't totally unexpected.

My dad had been in a nursing home, and his health had been deteriorating, so again, we were not taken totally by surprise. However, my husband's death was more than a body blow. He was a healthy and active man. We had no idea he had heart problems. The two of us had plans...

I don't really like talking or writing about the next few months. Never good at dealing with emotion, I coped with my grief by working long hours and sleeping very little. I don't think I was truly there for my two daughters, my mother and my mother-in-law who were also grieving. If I could live that time over again, I'd talk more about what I was feeling, and I'd spend more time helping my family deal with their feelings.

Yes, I may have felt I was in control of my own destiny before Huntley's death. His death taught me a hard lesson. There is no such thing as total control...and control is not as important as appreciating the moment, what we have right now, to its fullest.

By the time the next twelve months was over, I'd learned something else. I was ready to move on - needed to move on. I wasn't sure what I wanted, yet I began unconsciously searching.

Eventually I accepted a position at Upper Clements Park in the Annapolis Valley of Nova Scotia. In some ways it was similar to Kings Landing, yet in other ways very different. While Kings Landing was a loved and respected part of the New Brunswick landscape, and I felt very comfortable in my role there, Upper Clements Park was much more controversial, still struggling to be accepted into the provincial tourism community.

I liked the idea of the challenge. I felt I could help the people who worked there tell the world how truly wonderful Upper Clements Park was. I made the move.

I wanted the park to be a place where local people would come and bring their visitors. It took some convincing, but we finally got approval from government for free admission so people could come to the park and make up their own minds about it. A journalist whose name I can't remember gave me the slogan *Pay as you Play*. We dreamed up *Special Event Weekends*, and then every park employee, and especially my own staff, helped make those events successful. We had 250,000 bona fide visitors that first season I was there. We surveyed almost every visitor who came, and we had a satisfaction rating of over 98%.

We formed a local tourism group, made up of all the local attractions, so we could pool our resources and accomplish more together. Morning, noon and night, if the media called I was available, not just to talk about the park but about the whole area.

With my best friend, Anne, we explored Nova Scotia on my rare breaks from work. Since I practically lived at the Park, Anne got to know more people in town than I did, but together we became a part of the fabric of that community.

I was and am proud of what we accomplished at Upper Clements Park.

However, after three seasons, there were big changes at the park. I also felt Upper Clements Park had the support of the local community in a way that it hadn't when I first arrived. I knew it was time for me to leave.

While I was at Upper Clements Park, one of the local women asked if she could read my palm. She said, *Oh, my dear, you have had a hard life*. I was amazed at her words, because I didn't then, and I don't now, believe I've had a hard life. I've certainly worked hard. On the other hand, it really doesn't seem that much like work when you are doing what you want to do.

When I'd left teaching, years before, I'd said I wanted to go back to teaching some day, but the next time I'd like to teach adults. When I left Upper Clements Park, I was invited to become a part of Atlantic Region Management Training Centre as a facilitator, consultant and occasional assistant manager. I felt I'd come full circle.

Two years later, for the second time in my life, I became a small business owner. Together with a partner, we bought the assets of ARMTC, and became Parker, Boyd-Brown and Associates. In those early years, my business partner and I created a synergy neither of us could have accomplished on our own. We taught each other, supported each other and challenged each other. Eventually we parted ways, yet I am convinced we were both better at what we did because we did it together.

What is now PBBA Atlantic Inc. is by my measurements successful, and I believe there are still avenues to explore. Trainers, facilitators and speakers are a generous lot.

While few of us reach great material riches, there is a tremendous satisfaction in having the opportunity to share what we've learned over the years; to help the people who come to hear us speak use their own skills; and use their own wisdom to make their lives better.

For me, the most interesting aspect of this part of my journey is that I am almost exactly where I'd expected to be at this stage of my life, with very few exceptions. The landscape may have changed a bit, and I have a whole new set of colleagues to add to my list of friends, but I'm doing what I want to do...and that is "success" in my books.

I may not have chosen the road less travelled, but I have most definitely chosen the road. Whatever the outcome has been, I can never put the blame on others, because the decisions have been mine. On the other hand, any success I've had has most assuredly been helped along and made sweeter by other people in my life, particularly those I hold close to my heart.

My children are a big part of why I feel successful. I am tremendously proud of my two daughters. Each has carved out a career for herself quite different from anything I might have imagined for her. They too have had to find their own path. As a mother, my legacy to them has been roots and wings, and always my love and my support.

I have learned so much through the years, yet when it comes time to put words to paper, words seem so inadequate.

For the greater part of the last twenty-five years, I have kept a diary, chronicling the activities of my days. Not only has that diary helped me to win a great many arguments, it has also been a way to make certain no day is lost - that time does not pass me by or go unnoticed.

I have also been writing down yearly goals for myself since 1972. I do attribute those goals to helping me stay focused. I don't always reach these goals. Sometimes they change. Sometimes I no longer want them. Sometimes they've been delayed a little bit. If I'd been on track this book would have been finished about three years ago.

I attended a workshop a while ago that gave me some insight into why I think my goals have been a beacon for me. The facilitator said that some people move toward things they want and others move away from things they don't want. Those who move toward goals are sometimes seen by others as impossibly optimistic and naive. That describes me to a "T".

Not given to introspection, I've just set my goals and kept moving toward them. I still do have goals, by the way. I refuse to accept that the best is behind me. I still want to "just do it." I want to do, want to see and want to experience. I think Eleanor Roosevelt said it best,

The purpose of life, after all, is to live it, to taste experience to the utmost, to reach out eagerly and without fear for newer and richer experiences.

~ ~ ~

KAYE PARKER

Before Kaye created the training and consulting firm PBBA Atlantic Inc., Kaye had more than fifteen years of industry experience in management positions at the senior level, both in government and private sector. Her long public career has spanned many areas of interest.

She has been a teacher, a journalist and writer, a public relations and marketing specialist, and the producer of a successful television program. She uses her breadth of experience to design and deliver adult learning materials that are both practical and interesting.

Kaye has received recognition from every community in which she has worked, for her energy and dedication. She has also been a lifelong learner, with recognition of her work in public relations, human resources, recruiting and the speaking world.

Never Take No for an Answer

Eileen Pease

When I was a child, I saw a movie called *Never Take No for an Answer*. It was a simple tale, but I have never forgotten it, and its central message has been one of the most important drivers of my success.

It was about a small Italian boy with a sick donkey. The boy was convinced that if he could get his donkey into the crypt of Saint Francis of Assissi - the patron saint of animals - Saint Francis would cure his donkey. The film showed obstacle after obstacle the boy had to overcome, including arranging an audience with the Pope, to get his donkey into that crypt. By the end of the movie, he succeeded and his donkey was cured. Ever since, *Never Take No for an Answer* has been one of my mottos.

I always felt that if I wanted something enough, I could find a way to make it happen. As a very young child, I wanted to learn how to ride horses. I read books about horses, drew pictures of horses, and dreamed of the day when I would learn to ride. Our family did not have much money in those days, certainly not for luxuries like riding lessons. But one day, my mother took me to a jumble sale and we saw a pair of jodhpurs, a tweed riding jacket and a riding helmet all for a few shillings. They fit me perfectly and my dream came nearer.

Then my father found out that the daughter of one of his colleagues at work had a horse, lived near us, and was willing to give me some riding lessons for a small fee.

So I learned to ride on her horse Manuela, who was enormous, at least to me. I still have a photo of me sitting proudly on Manuela, just before the lesson on cantering. I was quite scared of cantering and Manuela probably felt my tension, because as soon as we started cantering, she bucked me off. After I got up and dusted myself off, I knew from my reading that I had to get back on her right away and canter again. I was very scared, but I did finally learn to sit down to her canter. For the rest of that week, I proudly showed off my bruises to anyone who would look at them.

Not long after that, we moved from England to Scotland and I met Janice Morrison, whose family had several horses on a small farm near our house. In exchange for helping out on both their horse farm and dairy farm, I improved my riding and Janice and I became close friends.

I didn't do well in school because I constantly worried about my mother. She had had her first nervous breakdown after my sister Alison was born, when I was just under two years old.

By the time I was ten years old, I had taken on a lot of responsibility for looking after my two sisters on the way to and from school (which involved shepherding them on and off a train, then a bus, and walking in between). Once I got home, I became quite vigilant in checking on how well my mother was and whether I had to continue looking after my sisters.

When I was leaving school, although I had the minimum qualifications to get into university, I did not want to struggle in that direction. I wanted to work with horses and to get the qualifications needed to do that. My father was not very pleased, but he said I could do it if I "did something sensible first." So I spent two years in college learning to be a secretary, before taking a year-long training course with horses. Even though I had much less experience than most of the trainees, I was determined to pass all the practical tests and exams. In fact, I passed all my exams and one of the examiners had been asked by friends to look out for a potential candidate to work on a small stud farm in Alberta, Canada. I was offered the job. At the same time, I was offered a home with a large show jumping stable near Melbourne, Australia, from which I could look for a job. I have often wondered what my life would have been like if I had gone to Australia.

But, I decided that a definite job and only a one-year commitment in Canada was better than a chance of a job and a two-year commitment to Australia. At the age of twenty, I emigrated to Canada.

Never take no for an answer served me well through the year I worked on a small horse farm just outside Calgary. By the end of that year, I decided that horses 24 hours a day, 7 days a week was not quite the life I wanted. I moved to Vancouver to look for a job that would allow me to earn enough money to buy my own horse. At one point, I figured out that school teaching would give me a good income and the summers off, so I worked to get into university.

The college I had attended in Scotland had grown into the University of Strathclyde, which looked good on my academic record.

I was accepted into the University of British Columbia and started by taking evening courses, while continuing to work during the day. In the meantime, I had become engaged to Alan, who was heading to Dalhousie University in Halifax to get his doctorate in Oceanography.

Using the never take no for an answer approach, I managed not only to gain entrance into Dalhousie University's first-year Biology and English courses starting in January, half-way through the university year, but I also obtained a full time job in the Registrar's office. A couple of years later, I learned to speed read and was able to get a job teaching speed reading for the

Evelyn Wood corporation. That job not only allowed me to attend university full time, but I managed to finish three years of university courses in two years and get a Bachelor of Arts and a Bachelor of Education at the same time.

After teaching reading as part of the elementary curriculum for five years, I returned to university to get a Master's degree in Education, specializing in reading. As I listened to one of my professors, Dr. Judith Newman, talk about how people learned to read, I realized that I understood a lot about reading from teaching speed reading. So I designed my own speed reading course and taught it first to Dr. Newman and a group of education students at Mount Saint Vincent University.

I taught my speed reading course as an evening course for the City of Halifax public education division, and then for the Extension Department of Dalhousie University, which later became Henson College.

Several people encouraged me to start my own business, which I thought was interesting, but I had no idea how to do that. After a few inquiries, I found that all I had to do was register a name with the Registry of Joint Stock Companies.

Just like that, I was the proud owner of a business called Dynamic Reading. Shortly after that, a friend of mine encouraged me to join the Halifax Board of Trade because she felt that more women should be on the Board of that august body. In those days, there were very few women business owners and even fewer who dared to join the board of trade. But I would not take no for an answer. Before long, I became a member of the board. Being on the board and chairing a committee turned out to be an incredible learning experience. I learned how business people thought. I learned to hire the best lawyer and the best accountant I could find, as I was told that they would always save me a lot more money than they ever cost me. I found that to be true, although the most expensive lawyer was not necessarily the best lawyer, as I found out some years later.

My business grew larger with more diverse offerings by me and from trainers I recruited, so I renamed it Dynamic Learning, which has achieved strong name recognition at this point.

I have faced many obstacles over the years, though, including divorce, having to raise my two sons on my own, and overcoming breast cancer, followed by a severe depression.

At that point, I had been in business for ten years and was just getting to the stage that the business was debt-free and producing a good income. The breast cancer was bad enough, but the depression was worse. I was back in hospital twice that year for a few weeks each time. As I was trying to put my life back together, I could feel myself going down again. I decided that I was the only person who was going to get myself well, so I set my goal to be healthy and happy and started pushing.

After my illness, I had to rebuild the business. Starting all over again was very, very hard. I had to motivate myself over and over again just to keep going, but I pulled out my old mantra from deep within - *never take no for an answer.*

Over the years, I have worried about not having a pension and not being able to build up an RRSP to the level I would have liked by now. But speed reading has always been a good steady seller. This year, I am working to develop a speed reading website through which I will teach people to speed read with a combination of teleseminars and support on the website. I know it will be breaking new ground, but I am convinced that it will be successful and that it will allow me to semi-retire in the next couple of years.

I am proud of the fact that I started a successful business with no money down and with very little experience, and that business has provided me with a good income for over twenty years. I have learned to have clear goals, to measure my progress towards those goals, to listen to expert advice, and to be persistent in the face of obstacles and difficulties. If I had to do it over again, I think I would have learned more about the potential of computers earlier than I did, and to have and work with more associates so that we could achieve more together than we could alone.

Besides reminding myself to *never take no for an answer*, I also take inspiration from the belief that luck occurs when preparation meets opportunity. If you do enough preparation, you find the opportunities. What other people might think of as luck, you know to be the result of creating the opportunities for yourself. Once I get my speed reading website earning enough money, I am going to re-connect with horses. Maybe then I will finally get to buy my own horse.

~   ~   ~

EILEEN PEASE

Eileen Pease is President of Dynamic Learning Inc., a company devoted to helping key people be more effective through learning. As a facilitator she has led executive, supervisory and management groups across Canada and the United States. Eileen is a senior consultant with MICA Management Resources (Toronto, ON) and is certified by the Management Research Group (Portland, ME) to facilitate their assessment-based development system in Leadership 360°™ and Strategic Leadership Practices™.

Eileen has been facilitating interaction within groups ranging from a few people to over 100 people since 1991. Her facilitation has been for as little as two hours, or as long as nine months. She has facilitated creative thinking, problem solving, strategic planning, and relationship sessions with front line employees, supervisors, managers, executives, and CEOs in homogenous and mixed groups.

Her two sons are now grown up and building great lives for themselves. In her spare time, Eileen paddles on a dragonboat team and enjoys gardening, being connected to horses, and reading.

Putting on a Good Face

Pam Robertson

I went to the woods because I wanted to live deliberately, to front only the essential facts of life, and see if I could not learn what it had to teach, and not, when I came to die, discover that I had not lived...
~ *Henry David Thoreau*, in *Walden, 1864*

My good friend mentioned recently that a lot had certainly changed in my life during the last couple of years. A divorce (my second), a son going to university, changing jobs, my parents both making it through cancer, crashing my car, and finally moving 5000 kms to live in the place that for a long time I had only been dreaming of. How did I do it, she wanted to know, without coming unglued? She needed to know because she was having trouble coping with things and felt like her own fine edge was coming unravelled.

I wanted to be really brave and make things look good, so initially I was tempted to tell her I am a resilient woman and that those things didn't "bother" me. In reality that wouldn't have been true, but it would have saved me a lot of explaining. Since I had made it through without going totally crazy, I thought that her question was worth some reflection not just so that I could answer her, but so that I could understand it too.

Change has been a central theme in my life for as long as I can remember. In my 42 years I have moved 21 times, lived in two different countries, three provinces and one territory, and five different cities.

I have been married and divorced twice, raised two children and worked in seven distinct occupational classifications. That kind of activity involves a lot of change, and also meant that I was outside of my comfort zone and introducing myself to new people, discussing or doing things that I was not used to, and sometimes putting on a good face for others to see.

I started putting on a good face when I was pretty young. My mom was not really a healthy mom and in those days if your back went out, the doctor sent you to bed for a week. When mom's back was bad, or for that matter when she was busy with other things, I looked after my little sister. She was three years younger than me, and in order to keep her happy I just needed to make sure that she had a full tummy and that her diaper was dry. My mom used to refer to me as her "mini-mom" and I responded by being the best little mom that I could be. When Dad came home from work he'd rub the top of my head and say what a great help that I'd been. As we got older and my mom went to work outside the house, I took on things like preparing dinner, ironing, and just trying to be helpful. That turned into hanging around the house a lot and Saturday mornings scrubbing the stove top or helping my dad build things in the garage. I thought that being family was pretty good, even on days when the routine seemed gut wrenchingly boring. I didn't see how things could be much different, nor did I really want them to be.

That's the way life was in those early years, kind of like a big pot of bland soup simmering on the back burner, waiting to have the seasoning kicked up. It stayed like that until I became obsessed.

You know how young kids today can become engrossed in video games or computers and they'll stay at it with such dedication that you wonder if they even remember to go to the bathroom? That's how I got with music, and music led to the army, and that changed my life forever.

My music career started out with recorder and then the ukulele craze hit in the mid 1970s. Every school had a ukulele group and some schools had several. The really good ones had students that travelled around and visited different cities, and they called it touring. Touring! They actually let you play these things all over the country. I went on tour with my ukulele group and my life became interesting, challenging and something worth getting excited about! Playing uke led to playing flute in junior high school and as soon as I played one I knew that I had found my instrument. I played every chance I got, including noon hours and after school band rehearsals. I practiced at home in my bedroom. I transcribed tunes off of the radio and played them.

I saved my babysitting money and my dad took me to National Music one Saturday afternoon and I bought my very own flute. No more having to rent one of the band instruments, I had one of my very own. That flute and I were inseparable, and as I neared the end of high school I wanted a better one, so off we went with the babysitting money again and I bought the flute of my dreams. I still have the receipt for that flute; in 1984 it cost $500 and it still sings beautifully.

That spring, while I was breaking in the new flute like a comfortable pair of slippers, I saw an ad in the paper that caught my eye.

I had been toying with the idea of attending music college after high school, but I didn't have the money for it and didn't know how I was going to get it. The ad said that a local army reserve unit was recruiting members for their marching band, and it was an ideal program for students who wanted to work full time in the summer, and then part time during the school year. Perfect! I could play flute and get paid for it all summer, and then have a part-time job during college! That I had to learn to march, shoot and clean a rifle probably couldn't hurt, I thought, and if that's what I had to do in order to play in the band, then that's what I would do.

Being a part of the army isn't for everyone, but for me it was great. I learned to be a stronger person because the army doesn't tolerate wimps. Joining the army was a huge step outside of my normal realm of activity and although I was competent musically, I really didn't have a whole lot of confidence in myself. I learned fast though, because I was really motivated. I learned how to march, how to shoot, and eventually I also learned to bark orders across the expanse of a parade square so that people could hear me. I found out that I could do a great job outside of my parent's home, and I embraced the transition that I knew was happening within me as I stood straighter, prouder, and stepped into a new way of living. I found out that I could be brave even though I wasn't what you'd call a courageous person or a risk taker when I first joined. I had gained enough competitive spirit in the musical world to know that I would succeed because in the army you either go big or go home, and that wasn't on my list of options. I realized that I *could* sleep in a shallow trench out in the middle of a farmer's field when I did it.

I learned that rappelling off of a tower was not a problem; I just had to trust the people that I was working with because we were all looking after one another. My knees were wobbling the first few times off that tower, but I made it. I survived.

Pushing myself to try new things - to appear brave in front of my peers whether I felt it or not - meant that when things did go bad in my life, I knew that I would get through it. At nineteen and now a corporal in the reserves, I found myself pregnant. My family doctor made an offer that I suppose many people could not refuse, but I wasn't about to abort a baby. I knew right then and in that instant that I could either resist the fact that I was pregnant, or I could embrace it. I told myself that since I was woman enough to get pregnant, I was also smart enough and resourceful enough to make it work. I celebrated a healthy pregnancy, and together with my family welcomed a daughter into my life.

It wasn't always easy. In fact sometimes it was really damned hard. Juggling work and child care, maintaining my position in the military while looking after my daughter - and new husband - was challenging, but I loved it. Being a mom in my own right and having a career felt great, right up to the point where it all came apart.

One evening the band was playing at a celebration on the base, and my husband was home with our 15 month old daughter. Since this was pre-cell phone days, I was startled to be called to the phone and knew as I reached for the receiver that something had to be horribly, terribly wrong

Our daughter, my husband stammered to me, had an accident in the bathtub, and I needed to meet them at the hospital. The paramedics were already with her at the house and getting her ready to load into an ambulance.

I left my flute behind, quickly explaining things to the band officer. I drove as quickly as I dared to reach the hospital in my little car, and actually had to pass the end of my own street on the way. Parked in front of the house I could see two fire trucks with lights flashing. My heart leaped higher into my throat, because I knew that the city only dispatched two fire trucks for a life threatening condition. I raced on to the hospital, anxious to catch up to the fleeing ambulance. Despite the years that have gone by, I can still remember running through the hospital hallways to the emergency department and looking for my little girl. My heavy black army boots thumped on the floor while my scarlet tunic flapped against my sides. When I was finally allowed to see my daughter, she was lying spread eagle on a gurney that looked enormous, her tiny elfin face pale against the white hospital sheets and tubes hanging everywhere. We were lucky for being so stupid, the emergency doctor assured us. She had been clinically dead and the paramedics were able to revive her. They had stopped the resulting seizures with medication so hopefully the brain damage would be minimal.

Someone else said how lucky we were that my husband was able to provide life saving CPR until the paramedics arrived. I was livid and speechless all at the same time!

He didn't save her, he nearly drowned her when he turned away to talk to someone on the phone while our little treasure was in the bath. Although she was on anti-seizure medication for a while and she still hates hospitals and doctors who insist on wearing white coats, our daughter did recover from her drowning. I celebrated her return, and our blessings, but I could no longer rejoice in my marriage.

By the time I got divorced, I had two children. I spent some time feeling miserable about the loss of my marriage. I had believed that marriage for us would be forever, but I could not move beyond what had happened and stay in that relationship. In my mini-mom days I would not have had the courage to leave my marriage; being a mom and part of a family was an ideal that I was shooting for from a very young age. Confidence and courage meant that I could make the changes that I needed, and despite choosing what might be the harder path sometimes, I get to live and celebrate my life as I have designed it. And that shows on my face.

~ ~ ~

PAM ROBERTSON

Pam Robertson has had many labels throughout her life including coach, consultant, manager, mom, musician, soldier and teacher.

She is a sought after writer and speaker because of her practical approach to people's life and career conundrums and her Ph.D. in career development. Pam has helped people from all walks of life - literally from accountants to zookeepers - and devotes her energies to writing, speaking and working with people who want to celebrate their lives. She has recently finished writing *Live Inspired! Create the Life of Your Dreams*, and is a contributor to the best-selling series *Wake Up and Live the Life You Love*. You can check out her website and link to her blog from www.mvpi.org.

CLIMB EVERY MOUNTAIN

DARLENE SANFORD

> *Climb Every Mountain*
> *Ford Every Stream*
> *Follow Every Rainbow*
> *Till You Find Your Dream*
> *~ Rodgers & Hammerstein*

> *With a Friend at Hand You Will See the Light*
> *If Your Friends are There then Everything's All right*
> *~ Elton John*

My name is Darlene Sanford and I am a triple D. The first time I remember demonstrating *Drive, Determination and Dedication* was when I was four years old. My mother and brother went to visit my grandparents approximately four miles away. I did not want to go at the time because I was riding my red and white tricycle up and down the cement walkway in front of the house. I was being my typical independent self. My father was in the backfield in the vegetable garden. I soon got bored of this activity, another behavioural trait, and I decided to set off for my grandparents. I do not recall the actual journey but I remember my soon to be uncle picking me up enroute after I had pedaled approximately two miles.

This included two steep hills and a bridge. I also remember the look on my Mother's face when we arrived and the look on my Father's face when we went home. (He was still in the garden.)

A child's dreams and inspirations need fostering to help achieve goals. I had overwhelming love and support from my parents Donald and Bessie Sanford. These two special people who have been married for fifty years have their priorities right in life. Brilliant individuals with many skills neither of them had the opportunity to finish high school. They wanted the best for their children. They wanted us to seize opportunities and fulfill our dreams. They are the first of many influential people who helped me foster my drive, determination and dedication. From them I learned by example.

Most of the memories of my childhood include time with family and creating goals and achievements. I grew up in Windsor Forks, Hants County, Nova Scotia. At eight years old after attending music class at school, I developed a burning desire to learn to play the piano. I promptly at the supper table that night announced that I wanted piano lessons. I remember going with my parents to buy a second hand piano for $150. According to our piano tuner, we purchased one of the best in the county. I took piano lessons for ten years and achieved Grade 9 Royal Conservatory.

As a child, I never remember being unhappy. My self—sufficient parents accomplished many things with little money. My first paycheque after university graduation was more than my father made as a carpenter and my mother (who was meant to be a mother) stayed home with us. We still got what we needed and most importantly lots of love and support. My parents were also 4-H leaders. I spent eight years in sewing, crafts, cooking and floriculture and learning leadership and public speaking skills.

My most memorable events were provincial shows and a citizenship trip to Ottawa where I went through a ceremony with twenty-one other people who were becoming Canadian citizens. I can still remember my speech and how proud I was to be a Canadian.

I am the eldest of three children. Paul is two years younger and Kimberley is nine years younger. As children, I took a leadership role. I often made up stories or re-enacted them from one of the many books that I had read. I always got Paul to play one of the characters. He conceded and has more patience than anyone I know. Kim was my "little" sister with whom I shared a room. She loved to come to my teenage parties and my friends all loved her. (Everyone still loves her.) As adults, my siblings are my friends and confidants. Paul and his wife Pam have two daughters, Alison and Mei Yin. Mei Yin was adopted from China was adopted from China. Kim and Geoff have two sons, Andrew and Matthew, with Abby and Max on the way. I love each and every one of them dearly. We are there for each other in times of joy and crisis. And yes we share drive, determination and dedication. Paul is an Industrial Engineer and Businessman and Kim is a Pharmaceutical Rep. We are fortunate to all live close by in Nova Scotia. I feel blessed.

My teenage years were filled with hard work to achieve high academic standards and filled with music. Brian Johnston, the Windsor Regional High School Band director, was my mentor. I played trombone and developed a taste for jazz. Our band even won a Canadian championship.

Music was so much a part of my life that I decided my career goal was to be a music teacher. I studied at Acadia University. After my first year, I knew something had changed. Music was and still is my passion. However, I missed academics. Hence, I commenced a search for "What will I do?". I had a high school classmate who wanted to be a physiotherapist. I saw an ad for volunteers needed in the Physiotherapy department in Kentville hospital. I volunteered two afternoons per week and worked in the department for the summer. I realized from this experience that I felt fulfilled working in physiotherapy. I switched to a biology major, convinced the Dean of Science to accept all my music credits as electives, and graduated from Acadia with a Bachelor of Science in Biology.

My drive, determination, and dedication kicked in to achieve my goal of becoming a physiotherapists. I recall the admission interview vividly. I relayed I was going to try every year until they let me in because I knew this was my career goal. As I started my physiotherapy training, I soon realized I had made the right choice. I developed a passion for every area of the profession early on.

I graduated from Dalhousie University in 1985 and went to work at the Victoria General Hospital in intensive care. As a young woman I was exposed to many devastating injuries and learned an appreciation for living life to the fullest for you do not know what tomorrow brings. I also learned to work in a team of highly trained professionals.

I became the Atlantic Physiotherapy representative for the Canadian Lung Association and enjoyed a six-year term including the role of president and board member. As well as learning about a national organization I also learned how surrounding yourself with people who share your drive, determination and dedication produce an accomplished effective team. I worked with physiotherapists from across the country who will be my lifelong friends and colleagues and traveled to many cities in all provinces of the country.

So focused on goals, career, and my family I never put much emphasis on dating. The boy who took me on a date on my sixteenth birthday became my husband nine years later. Our lives evolved together through university and career and we moved to Lunenburg in 1988 so my husband could start his own computer business. We created and operated a dinner theatre and I became director of physiotherapy at Fisherman's Memorial Hospital. My resistance to leave Halifax quickly vanished as I met the friendly effective team at FMH and began treating the warm people of Lunenburg County. Lunenburg soon became my community and felt like home.

December 13, 1991 was the most special day in my life. My son, Brandon Leslie O'Leary was born. I added love, admiration, and motherhood to drive, determination and dedication. Brandon became the focus of my life.

1995 was my year of trials and tribulation. My family upbringing, which included regular attendance at our Anglican Church and Sunday school, taught me trust, respect, and faith.

I learned that year that life can be full of lies, deceit and manipulation and how people will attack you when you are vulnerable. The breakup of my marriage was one of the struggles I faced at that time and I faced a mirage of emotions and life realizations. I learned what was important in life: Health, Happiness, Family and Friends. The overwhelming support from my family and many dear friends got me through this time.

The challenges in my life however seemed immaterial because my dear friend and colleague, Kelly Bang was dying of cancer. Kelly was an occupational therapist who asked me to become part of her business. In my practice through continuing education and experience, I was developing as a physiotherapist but I was searching for more ways to help my patients. Kelly taught me the functional approach to physiotherapy - assessing movement performance during life activities. She was ahead of her time and an avid reader and thinker. We shared the same philosophy. Her last career wish was for me to carry on the business.

My physiotherapy clinic, Nova Functional Assessments and Therapy Services, Kelly's vision, has become my passion. It is a multidisciplinary clinic including physiotherapy, occupational therapy, massage therapy, and psychology. I have devoted my life to providing Physiotherapy to the people of Lunenburg County. I have many people to thank for helping me make this happen. I was the physiotherapist at Dr. William Stanish's orthopaedic clinic at FMH for 11 years. He shared my drive, determination, dedication, and passion for helping patients live a better quality of life.

As well as sharing his wealth of knowledge and expertise he became a supporter of my skills and gave me the encouragement I needed to take over and grow the private practice. We became a team, along with Rosemary Smith, organizer extraordinaire, bringing a high standard of orthopaedic treatment to the people of Lunenburg County. He will always be my colleague and my extraordinary distinguished friend.

I extend heartfelt thanks to each member of my strong professional team at Nova. Each one of them demonstrates the drive, dedication and determination to achieve excellence. When I hire new staff, the most important thing that I look for is how that individual will fit in with the "dream team".

Another individual who has a strong influence on my life is Dr. Diane Wilson. Diane is a Rheumatologist who moved her office into my clinic when she first moved to Lunenburg. She shared my passion for getting to the root cause of a problem - not just treating symptoms. I truly believe in health care this is the recipe for success. Diane and I participate in a weekly clinic jointly assessing patients with multiple musculoskeletal issues and pain to diagnose the root cause. We then can give the patients goals and treatments to improve their quality of life.

In 1997, I purchased a property in which to live and operate the business. This was economical and allowed me to be close to my son. In true community spirit patients would bring their children to play with Brandon while they were receiving treatment. I hired Juanita Corkum for a babysitter. Juanita became a member of our family.

She is a widow who brought up four children of her own and just retired when she turned 65. Her reliability, dedication and love made life much easier for us.

One of the things I marvel at is how people who come for treatment with pain can have so much fun. Every day we hear entertaining stories. Like the two women in their 60's who started discussing their old boyfriends when unbeknownst to them one of them was in the next cubicle. I originally started work at 8:30 a.m. Since many of the injured workers were early risers, they would congregate on my doorstep an hour early for a "chinwag". I pushed up my start time but the trend continued. I refused to start earlier than 6:30 a.m. and had to forbid earlier arrival. In my practice, one of my most satisfying moments is when the pain goes away and I see my patient smile for the first time. I then find out who they really are.

My continuing goal is to evolve to fulfill the physiotherapy needs of all sectors of my community. We have satellite clinics in some of the local industries to address the needs of the injured worker and provide educational seminars. I am a co-owner of Lacewood Physiotherapy with Gillian Lirette in Halifax, Nova Scotia. Ergonomics, muscle imbalance and acupuncture have become my specialty areas through extensive postgraduate study. My passion for physiotherapy continues to evolve. I will always thank Kelly Bang who created Nova Functional Assessments and Therapy Services for paving this road for me.

Our mutual friends often comment, *If Kelly could see you now!* What is special for me now is Kelly's daughter Klee has just come to work for me as a massage therapist. She has her mother's zest for life.

I have saved the best for last. My son Brandon and I have a special bond. We share a passion for music and perform together regularly, most recently at my sister's wedding. I never had to encourage him to practice piano. Even at six years old, he practiced an hour daily. He has just completed his Grade 7 Royal Conservatory. He plays his alto saxophone in the Tuesday Night Big Band in which I have played my trombone since 1986. He is now becoming part of my musical family and friends. Brandon and I belong to the South Shore Players, he as an actor and singer, and I am musical director and pianist. We participate in the Christmas musical production each year.

Early in his schooling, Brandon was diagnosed with ADHD. We had many school meetings to determine what was right for him. Working as a team with an occupational therapist, principals, teachers, an accomplished teacher's assistant, school psychologists, and Brandon and I was what allowed him to achieve success. It was soon apparent that my son was easily bored and had to be constantly stimulated. I am so proud of him. He has learned to channel his excess energy into his passions - music, mathematics, history, wrestling and swimming. He has developed drive, determination, dedication and excellence. My lesson for anyone is exposing your children to many activities so they can find their passions.

Again, my ongoing family support from my parents and siblings, Brandon's Godparents and my friends helped me get through the hard times. I also thank my dear friend George Wawin for his love, support and dedication. He has helped me with my vision of what is right for my son. He and his family have become part of mine.

Some of my most treasured moments with Brandon are our travels. His first trip with me was to a Physiotherapy Lung Association meeting when he was six weeks old. I spent a month in New Zealand backpacking and visiting a friend with Brandon on my back when he was almost two years old. I still remember him feeding the sheep.

I promised him when he was four years old I would take him to Disney World when he was eight and he held me to it. We also went to Florida this year. When he was twelve years old, we went to Singapore, Bali and Malaysia. We lived with friends, traveled and I studied acupuncture. In Malaysia, we visited my university roommate whom I had not seen for twenty years. We got to live with her and her Chinese family and experience the food and the culture. It was an incredible experience for both of us.

My son has a passion for genealogy and history. His O'Leary ancestors had been Chieftains in Ireland in the 1500's. We went to Ireland in 2006 and found their last remaining castle. I still recall the directions. *"Get yourself to Inchigeelagh (one hour from Cork), go to the Creedons Hotel and ask for Joe. He will give you directions to the castle."*

And then off we went from there two miles through open green fields and rolling hills of cows and sheep to find the castle. I will never forget the look on my son's face with the first glimpse and reading his detailed article of what used to be in the castle while we went through it.

So, what lies ahead? Nothing but opportunity to use my drive, determination and dedication. My son wants our next trip to be to Japan. I will always call Nova Scotia home. The word failure is no longer part of my vocabulary.

I have learned that things that change beyond my control in life can only lead to the next opportunity and challenge. I have so many things I want to experience. My advice: Seize opportunities and utilize resources - namely people. Find common goals so everyone can work together as an effective team. Surround yourself with positive people whom you love and respect. Treasure and love your family and friends and communicate often. Life only gets better if you let it.

～　～　～

DARLENE SANFORD

Darlene is proud to call herself a native Nova Scotian, born in Windsor in 1961.

No matter where her travels take her she is proud to call Lunenburg home, where she lives with her son Brandon. Darlene is owner of Nova Functional Assessments and Therapy Services Ltd., a multidisciplinary rehabilitation clinic employing physiotherapists, occupational therapists, psychologists and dedicated support staff. She graduated from Acadia University with a BSc in biology and from Dalhousie University with a BSc in physiotherapy. Her special interests are in muscle imbalances, chronic pain and ergonomics.

Besides being a proud Mom and business owner Darlene has a passion for music. She plays trombone in the Tuesday Night Big Band and is pianist and musical director for the South Shore Players. She treasures time with family, friends, and loved ones and never loses touch with the people that mean the most. She is honoured to have been chosen to be involved in this book and to have developed a connection with such talented women.

Risk!

Sharon Skaling

Risk! Risk anything! Care no more for the opinions of others, for those voices. Do the hardest thing on earth for you. Act for yourself. Face the truth.
~ Katherine Mansfield

When the Halifax Metro Chamber of Commerce named me as a business innovator and risk-taker, I was surprised. I had never thought that how I run my life and my business was innovative - until I realized that I have been taking risks all my life. I believe that it has been through taking risks that I have been successful - I just jump in with both feet, eyes squeezed shut, and hope for the best. Fortunately, I also work hard at being the best I can be, treating others well, and the best has come to me.

I think the first risk I took that affected my business career was moving from Halifax, NS to Vancouver, BC at the age of twenty. Fresh out of university, $500 in my pocket, knowing one person in Vancouver, and not so much as a job interview lined up. All I had was an incredible determination to work for the T. Eaton Company and to be accepted into their Management Training Program.

This program was only offered in Toronto and Vancouver, and, as I did know *one* person in Vancouver, that became my destination. Plus, they have those great mountains out there!

Through great perseverance, I was hired by Eaton's and was accepted into the program before the end of my first year of employment. I had the good fortune of working for a supervisor and department manager who recognized my skills and talents, even though my shyness tried to hide them. They helped me to develop my confidence and supported me in reaching my destination. By working both as a salesperson on the floor and as a buyers assistant for ladies' wear, I learned how to work with others, how to be an effective manager, and how to see my dream of working at Eaton's and in the fashion industry come true. My hard work and relationship skills paid off when the company restructured their buying practices, changing from regional buying to central, based out of Toronto. I was one of a handful in the office that was asked to stay on during the transition and act as liaison between the Pacific Mainland and head office. No longer working in the actual buying process, I became the main contact for the seven lower mainland store ladies' wear supervisors and staff for all issues relating to receiving merchandise, inventory, sales and promotions, and troubleshooting problems.

I then worked with the buyers in Toronto, via telephone, to resolve issues, provide feedback, and assist in their understanding of how and what our customers were looking for. In retrospect, I realize that this was the first time that I saw that my approach brings me success. From hundreds of buyer's and administrative assistants who had been working at the location at the time, I was one of approximately twenty-five who were kept on.

My approach includes having respect for my customers, colleagues and managers, working hard and long hours when required, and having a clear vision of what I want. I believe that these are key characteristics of a successful person, and ones that I am grateful for having been developed during this time in my life, as I would certainly need to call on them many times in my lifetime.

During the three years that I lived in Vancouver, I managed to find time in my very hectic schedule of working full-time and participating in the Management Training Program to marry a young man, who was also from Nova Scotia. He was articling at one of the major Chartered Accountant firms in Vancouver, so our life was one of very little time together as we both devoted a great deal of time to our careers. C.A. firms started to lay-off their articling students, as there was a glut of students and not enough work.

My husband was one of those students and we were faced with the challenge of his losing his credits-to-date unless he found employment. I made the decision to leave Eaton's, and Vancouver, so he could continue his career development through his father's C.A. firm in Nova Scotia. While I had found that success had come easily in my career, it was time to find it elsewhere.

A few years later I found myself living in a small community with two children and in an unhappy marriage. I had sacrificed my career for my husband's and discovered that I needed things that this lifestyle could not provide - a challenging career, a partner who could be present in the relationship, and a frequent "hit" of city life.

As I continued to live without these things, my body began to show signs of stress, and I began to sink further into a depressive state of mind. As with so many people who are affected by depression, I found it difficult to take care of my children and myself. My son now tells me that he remembers that I was angry, sad, and in physical pain. And that so very accurately sums up how I was feeling at the time. As part of a 'rescue Sharon' plan, which I had no idea of the final outcome, I returned to school at the Nova Scotia Community College and received the Governor General medal and awards for the highest marks in the business program.

How I had managed to juggle raising a family, attending classes, and achieving these honours somewhat amazes me. Meanwhile, my marriage was falling apart at the seams and I knew that if I didn't take action, I would die. Not physically, but in every other sense of the word. So…time to take another risk.

On my 35th birthday, I left my husband and our eight and ten-year old children and moved over 200 km away to start my life over. Weakened both mentally and physically, I slowly began to take my own life back. Living apart from my children is definitely the hardest thing that I have ever done. Good mothers don't leave their children. And yet, I did. Or so it may seem. I knew that the person who was leaving them was not their mother, and the only way that I could ever re-gain myself was to leave. The children had a secure home life with after-school care, friends and family whom I knew would take care of them as I recovered.

I again sacrificed my needs for someone else's, my children, and while I wish it could have been different, I do not regret my decision. As I slowly gained my strength and self-confidence again I was able to show my children who their mother really was. It was another risk that paid off.

The experience of being an absentee parent helped me be stronger, more resilient, and able to take even more risks…life goes on no matter how hard it seems at the time.

The reward has been immeasurable. My children are strong and confident individuals who are following their own paths in their choices for education and careers. They will create their own success.

Shortly after I moved, I began working in the dental administration field. I started out as a part-time recall clerk and within three years I was managing a large dental practice, where I stayed for four years. I believe that getting through the experience of leaving my children and seeing them for only two weekends a month, of not living with my son since he was eight years old (my daughter came to live with me four years after I left the marriage), and living every day missing them and their lives has taught me many personal lessons that I was able to transfer to my business life, and can be used by anyone in any level of business. I really believe these lessons have helped me be more successful with owning and running my own business and are lessons that I will never forget. The three key areas of learning for me were setting priorities, decision-making, and being a parent.

From each of these I believe there are lessons that translate to any relationship, not just as an entrepreneur.

Setting priorities: When my children were with me, nothing was more important. I did not go out with friends or do anything that did not involve them. From Friday evening until Sunday afternoon, they were it. And they treated me the same way.

The Lesson: In business, and in life, treat the people you are with as the most important thing in your world at that moment. Whether you are on the phone, in a one-on-one meeting, or chatting over dinner, treat others with respect and interest.

There is never a risk when you treat others with respect. The risk is when you forget to treat yourself with respect. I learned the hard way that constantly putting others' needs in front of your own is damaging to self-respect and self-confidence. I am still working on recognizing how important I am and valuing the time I spend on myself. I think that is one reason why I have chosen to remain single right now, as I learn more about how to care for and love myself.

Decision Making: As the children's lives got busier, I allowed them to make decisions for themselves in respect to when they were with me. They needed to feel that they could decide to attend a sleepover instead of staying with me, to be actively involved with their friends, and not feel guilty about their decision.

My son become very involved with hockey and played most weekends. That experience taught him so much about leadership and team development. Not seeing him for weeks on end was worth it as I could see his personal growth.

The Lesson: Allow others, whether employees or co-workers, your child's sport coach, or your partner, to make decisions themselves - discover their needs and strengths and work with them to develop what they do best. As the sole proprietor of a small business I recognize my talents and skills and developed them while contracting others to do what I could not or did not want to do. Trying to be everything to everyone just doesn't work. Be your own person and believe in who you are and what you do. And, trust that it is okay to change what you do when you want to.

Being a Parent: I learned a valuable lesson through my son - that I didn't need to physically be in his life every day to have an influence on him. He chose the best time to share that with me at his high school graduation during his salutatory address while thanking his grandparents, his father, and me for the skills he had learned from each of us. He also showed me the humorous side of his personality as he thanked me "for teaching me how to treat a girl like a lady" and his girlfriend for "teaching him what happened when he did not listen to his mother." I was certainly one of the proudest mothers in the room that night!

The Lesson: People do not need to be micro-managed to do the job.

When you have the right people for the job and they are trained with the appropriate skills they will be successful in their own right. Successful leaders and managers are always encouraging others to be successful. I believe there is more personal risk in trying to "do it all", than in working with others to do what they are talented at.

In 2001 at the age of 42, I found myself without an employment contract and time to evaluate what I wanted to do when I "grew up". There was much analysis of self, what I had enjoyed from previous jobs, (what I did not like too), and what I loved to do as a kid. I believe that often what we wanted to be when we were kids is what we should look at as a career choice. I have always loved clothes and fabrics, helping people be their best, and running my own show. I found a title that met my wants and needs and, most importantly, my passion to help others in Image Consulting. I explored the possibilities, took the training I needed in Toronto, and formed my first company.

Even after all this training and desire to work as an Image Consultant, I got scared of taking this huge step into the world of entrepreneurship and the unknown.

My daughter was in high school, there were bills to pay, and I just could not justify taking such a huge leap of faith. While I was familiar with the benefits of taking risks, this one was just too great a risk at the time. So I accepted an offer as a spa director for a new spa in Halifax. I had the opportunity to develop my image consulting venture in the spa, as it became one of the services we offered.

I thought I would gain new skills and knowledge in an area that would assist me in the future. And I was right - I am very grateful for that experience. Sometimes we have to look at what we gain, rather than what we might lose.

It was a year later that I made the decision to fully embrace the risk of owning my own image consulting business, and I jumped with both feet into a full-time operation. I hired a marketing firm, and we were designing business cards, brochures, and a marketing plan. My life changed overnight and it was happening - my dreams of working in the fashion industry, on my terms, were coming to life.

One of the most important things that I credit my success to is this - I now believe in myself. I believe that my life experiences, while not always the experiences I would have asked for, are what have made me who I am. That belief carries me through situations that I would never have imagined myself to go through.

The dream and the belief persevere, and so do I. I do not believe in limitations and I carry on with confidence and love for what I do.

It is also important to know what motivates you, because it is easy to become disillusioned, overwhelmed, and defeated. Some of my key motivators are survival, financial security, the desire to achieve, succeed, and help others while fulfilling my need to be creative.

When you understand what motivates you, you can feed that need and it becomes easier to carry on with your purpose.

Recently, I have taken another risk that I know is one of the most important stages for my business and for me personally. Success does not come from being stagnant but rather from constantly adjusting to trends and personal shifts while staying true to your values and standards. I made the decision to take the risk of publicly speaking about a time in my life that I tried desperately to keep hidden from my family, friends, employers and employees. Before I had regained my self-confidence and faith in myself, I was in a second marriage: A physically and emotionally abusive marriage that totally enveloped my life.

Every time I attend a meeting on domestic violence or talk about my experiences, I take the risk of being sought out and hurt again by him. It is a risk that I am willing to take.

As a survivor of domestic violence, I feel strongly about helping other women find the strength and courage that I did to escape. While I thought that I could forget that time in my life, I have come to realize that I have a skill as a speaker that I must use to reach others in similar situations. If my experiences can help even one woman gain the confidence and courage to improve her life, then I will continue on. With the same respect and integrity that I have used with my first company, I formed a second company that focuses on speaking and reaching even more people with my message of hope for the future.

I love what I do. I am so passionate about the difference that I make that it provides all the encouragement that I need to carry on. When you truly follow your heart, love and believe in what you do, and share your skill and knowledge with others you are a success. The best part is not when you see that in the reflection of your children, your clients, and your community but when you embrace success as your own.

Taking risks by, as Katherine Mansfield so boldly stated, *"Do the hardest thing on earth for you. Act for yourself. Face the truth."* That has allowed me to constantly strive to be the best me that I can be, and to help others in their quest to uncover their inner selves and express it to the world. And I just can't find any risk in that!

Always a risk-taker, I find balance in my life through yoga, meditation, and the support of my friends.

Love. Gratitude. Hope.

~   ~   ~

SHARON SKALING

Sharon Skaling, president of *Total You* and *Panoply 3D image Consulting Inc.* is an innovative leader in the areas of personal branding and perception management.

Sharon has been featured for her entrepreneurial and innovative business development in numerous business papers and journals, including *Progress Magazine* and received the 2005 Sobey School of Business *Leader of Tomorrow* award for demonstrating exceptional initiative, visibility, resourcefulness, and involvement in the business community in Atlantic Canada.

The coaching/consulting process that she uses was developed over a lifetime of learning. It incorporates the disciplines of Image consulting, personal branding, business etiquette, and life/ business coaching.

Sharon has published three books - her latest, *You: The Total Package*, was released in October 2008.

Sharon was the 2007 President of the Canadian Association of Professional Speakers (CAPS) Halifax Chapter and is the current Board President of Dress for Success Halifax.

Following my Dreams - My Journeys to Success

Nancy Sparks

Some time ago, I came to a realization, which I wrote out as a positive affirmation. I often repeat it to myself, and share it with others when I can: *Success is when you realize that your dreams, abilities, life experiences and perseverance have allowed you to gather inner strength during adversity.* To realize that this success has brought you satisfaction along your continuous journey of life.

I've also come to realize my journey of life has actually been a series of smaller journeys. Each one has had its own challenges and successes, and all have combined to make me the person I am today. My first journey began when I was born premature at eight and a half months. I often heard stories about how my parents, Henry and Bessie Sparks, prayed for me to live. Looking back, it's clear that God had a purpose for me, which allowed me to survive. He also granted me a solid foundation for success - the love and guidance of my parents.

I recall how, as a young girl growing up in the African Nova Scotian community of Lake Loon/ Cherry Brook, my parents nurtured and exposed me to many role models, places and experiences. In this way, they provided me with a belief system that prepared me for success. My parents often told me that a good education is the key that unlocks the door to a wealth of career opportunities.

They stressed the importance of humility - the idea that other people would help me reach my goals. Most of all, they reminded me to stay focused on my dreams. I drew strength from their words and believed that I could succeed at anything I did.

My budding faith was tested on my first day at school - the beginning of my academic journey. I was very apprehensive about leaving my mother. My fears only began to subside when my Grade Primary teacher, a lady from Jamaica who was also the school principal, took me by the hand and told me that, "everything was going to be alright." She gave me an abacus to play with. As I slid those pretty balls back and forth, I knew I was going to be a teacher, and that I would demonstrate the same kindness and attention to my students that she had shown me.

Many teachers would follow, each one from a different cultural background. Yet all had one thing in common - they took an interest in me. Not just in my academic well being, but also my social and emotional welfare. Through their encouragement, and the support of my parents, I continued to do well in school. It wasn't always easy; I made many sacrifices to maintain good grades.

I studied while other children played and completed assignments instead of watching television. Though I didn't realize it at the time, I was developing self-discipline - the focus I would need to succeed. There were setbacks along the way. My dreams of being a teacher were briefly shattered by a guidance counsellor who told me I should pursue another career choice.

His exact words were *"You people would be better off going to vocational school."*

I couldn't believe what he had said and told my parents. Having great faith in the education system, they thought there must have been a misunderstanding. Yet before they could arrange a meeting to discuss this situation, my social studies teacher, who had always been supportive of my career plans, intervened. He provided me with applications for local universities and student loan information. Thanks to his help, I was not only accepted at every university where I applied, I also received a scholarship. Once again, someone had lent a helping hand at the right time; my dreams were still within reach.

After graduating high school, a new journey began, one that took me to Mount Saint Vincent University and into the Bachelor of Arts and Bachelor of Education Degree programs. It was an opportunity to put all the lessons I learned at home to good use. For two years, I lived in residence and discovered the importance of being my own person, staying focused on my goals and pursuing my studies while still spending time with family and friends. These were challenging yet rewarding years. Unlike the public schools I attended, I was the only person of colour in many of my classes. This may have been intimidating for some people, but not for me, and it gave me the chance to put the social skills I had learned into practice. I made many friends as a result, and some of these friendships have continued to this day. It also helped that I had progressive professors. In fact, one encouraged me to write a research paper on my heritage – *Blacks in Canada*.

Working on that paper not only gave me pride in who I am, it allowed me to share my culture and history with others who may not have experienced it before.

After graduation, I hit a roadblock. There was a surplus of teachers in Nova Scotia, and many were leaving the province to find work. I was determined to stay here and follow my dreams, but with no employment and a student loan to repay, things looked pretty bleak. Nevertheless, I knew things would work out if I continued to have faith and persevered. One day, my dad, a mason with his own business, asked if I would like to work with him while I waited for substitution positions. I jumped at the chance. This was a time in my life when things like manicures and makeup were not part of my lifestyle. So the opportunity to mix cement, pass bricks and sweep dusty basements was a welcome one. What's more, it was a chance to make money and spend time with my dad.

It turned out to be a memorable year. Apart from two calls for substitution, it was the last full year I spent with dad before he passed away. I learned work and life skills that I continue to draw on. Moreover, I learned that even if your dreams are delayed, you can stay positive and productive. You can take each challenge and turn it into an opportunity.

Just before my dad passed away, I was hired as a public school teacher - the fulfillment of my lifelong dreams. The fact that I could share this with my dad, and hear him say how proud he was of me, is a memory I will always cherish. I loved being a teacher.

My students gave me a sense of purpose, and I became a role model to them by sharing my experiences and life lessons. One former student later told me that I had inspired her to become a teacher; another said I had encouraged her to be a mortician simply by telling her she could accomplish any goal she set her mind to through honesty, hard work and doing her best.

These wonderful memories have given me inner strength during troublesome times, and reminded me that success is knowing that you have given meaning to someone's life other than your own.

My journeys continued, taking me from the classroom to administrative positions with the Halifax County-Bedford District and Halifax Regional School Boards. Despite the change in job titles, teaching has remained part of my life. I've taught mediation and conflict resolution skills to school staff and students, and today I provide teachers with strategies and skills for choosing and delivering learning materials in regional classrooms as Curriculum Advisor. I am also involved in policy introduction, implementation and professional development sessions. The lessons, skills and inspiration I've received from the many role models in my life continue to guide me, contributing to my success and contentment, both professionally and personally.

There is another journey that has had a great impact on my life and made a significant contribution to my success. It's a journey of spirituality that was inspired by a realization that there is more to life than having a good job, a family and friends. Though I was raised in a Christian home, I did not have a personal relationship with God.

I spent many years asking myself questions such as: With all that I have achieved in life, why do I feel as if something is missing? Why do I often feel an emptiness that nothing seems to fill? I was trying to make sense of my life. After years of constant praying and asking God to help me answer these questions, He finally did. The moment of clarity came during my aunt's funeral; I felt a sense of freedom, a weight being lifted from my soul. I told my cousins about my experience and they said that their mother had been praying that I would become a child of God before she passed away.

This unique relationship with God brought my life to a place unlike any I'd experienced before, one of incredible joy. My mom, whose prayers and patience that I would know the grace of God had finally been rewarded. We had a day of celebration, and the highlight came when she escorted me to the baptismal waters. My only regret was that my dad was not there to share in this moment. Nevertheless, my spiritual awakening has filled my life with new meaning and purpose.

Through her faith, determination and perseverance in times of trouble, my mom has had a great impact on my life. Her hope in the face of uncertainty is an example I've tried to follow, and has provided me comfort in some of my darkest moments. It was this unwavering sense of faith and hope that saw me through one my biggest challenges yet - the decision to place my mom in a nursing home following her diagnosis of dementia. When I visit her, I still see her strength, positive attitude and wisdom shining through. As I explore my own successes, I reflect on and find strength in mom's character and values.

I am blessed to have had her and so many other great role models in my life to help me follow my dreams. Thanks to their constant encouragement and kindness, I am living my life to the fullest, always focused on what is good. I surround myself with positive and caring people, who help me stay grounded and serve as new role models for me.

Though my journeys have been many, I continue to seek out new paths in my career, my community and my spirituality. In my church, I have become a member of the Missionary Society and Education Committee. I am also involved with a group that teaches life skills to youth based on Christian principles. In my community, I volunteer with Seniors and Youth groups. I have served as President and Vice President of the Board of Directors for the Nova Scotia Home for Coloured Children. Through church and community work, I've shared my experiences with - and gained insight from - people young and old. I am honoured to have touched their lives and, in turn, have received personal satisfaction and appreciation through my relationships with them.

Looking back on where I've been, and ahead to where I am going, I realize we were all put on this earth for a reason. How we choose to use our gift of life is up to us. I choose to live, love, laugh, cry and to make a difference. I would like to leave a legacy that will echo my accomplishments and humility. I want only for those who have come into contact with me to say, "It is a blessing to have known her." By following my dreams, I hope I will achieve this measure of success in my life. Until then, my journeys continue.

~   ~   ~

Nancy Sparks

Current position: Race Relations, Cross Cultural Understanding and Human Rights Program Advisor, Halifax Regional School Board.

Previous positions with the Halifax Regional and Halifax County Bedford District School Boards, classroom teacher, area liaison officer, facilitator, resource and community coordinator, sexual harassment coordinator, acting supervisor, race relations, cross cultural understanding and human rights department.

Co-authored article, *Identifying Bias in Resource Materials,* Canadian Library Association.

Participated in video productions, *Black Studies: A Model, Freedom Of Information and Protection of Privacy Act,* Department of Education and *The Little Black School House,* produced and directed by Dr. Sylvia Hamilton.

Received Bachelor of Arts and Education, Mount Saint Vincent University, Master of Education, Saint Mary's University.

Member of the Cherry Brook United Baptist Church. as Deaconess, Women's Missionary Society, Education Committee, and Supervisor of the Baptist Youth Fellowship Group.

MAKING CONNECTIONS

MICHELLE STRUM

When we seek for connection, we restore the world to wholeness.
Our seemingly separate lives become meaningful as we discover how
truly necessary we are to each other.
~ Margaret Wheatley

As I grow older, I become more aware of how deep my need is for a sense of connection. When I feel connected, be it to myself, my peers or my work, it seems my life and its daily routine is easily tackled. However, when I feel a sense of disconnect, I struggle, virtually unable to complete even the easiest of tasks.

I was born on April 1, 1977 in Blockhouse, Nova Scotia. My Dad was a fisherman and my mom a secretary. Raised as a hard worker, my father chose to spend his time at home farming and logging, even though his work kept him away from us most weeks. As the eldest of two sisters, I prided myself on my ability to help Dad do the chores involved in cultivating crops and animals. I loved learning new things and was really proud when I completed a task well. I especially enjoyed being involved in my parents' work because I loved the sense of bonding and community that existed in the workplace.

From an early age, I prided myself on being strong, independent and determined. Though always eager to help my parents, my mom remembers me as a child who wanted to do things my way.

This led to a few arguments, yet Mom remembers fondly the times I would surprise her with a new trick or task I learned on my own.

My self-motivation, work ethic and desire to be a part of something made me an overachiever in elementary school. I worked hard, pushing myself to earn high grades, be part of as many clubs as possible and be the lead role in the play. New experiences, instead of daunting me, excited me as they presented opportunities for accolades and unique connections. Looking back, I think most of the things I did so effortlessly then would be more terrifying for me today. I believe I was so excited by the feeling of task completion and achievement that I didn't stop to consider my fears. For example, I was six when I began figure skating. I practised three times a week until I was 17. The feel of flying through the air on smooth ice is something I still thoroughly enjoy today.

As I transitioned into junior high school, my interest in extracurricular activities and good grades waned considerably. Instead of feeling challenged, I felt pressured to conform to authority, and a disconnection. Before, I believed that I was an essential part of school, as if my successes helped validate the system. By the age of 12, I felt like I was being made to do things that I found myself questioning and, ultimately, resisting.

By the time I entered senior high, I felt as if I were on a downward spiral. My disinterest and "bad attitude" had led to pretty low grades and fewer choices for university. At the time, I didn't care. The whole process of graduating high school and entering university seemed skewed.

I had been told that if you were smart, you took science, and if you didn't know what you wanted to do with your life, you took arts. But science? What was that about anyway? I didn't know what kind of job I wanted or could get. To be honest, I really wasn't even focused that far in advance. I was disengaged and, in many ways, I had become negative.

I remember sitting at Bob's Café in Bridgewater, looking at my acceptance and rejection letters from universities, trying to decide how to use the next few years of my life. I was disenchanted. The letters seemed like a joke, none promising anything appealing to me. My friend Julie was with me, casually pondering her future and contemplating overseas travel. When I heard her mutter New Zealand, I countered, "What about Australia?"

Barely five minutes later we were using the café's courtesy phone to tell our parents we were going to Australia. Like most of my decisions then, I had no idea of the true implications of my choice. Obviously, my family was shocked - I was raised to be the family's first university graduate. But I had other plans.

Even if it had been a long-held dream, deciding to move to Australia was big. My parents couldn't understand why I had to go to the country that was geographically farthest from our hometown. At the time I'm not sure I did either, but I can say now that my highest priority was taking control of my life; I needed to do something I had chosen to do.

So off to Australia I went with $2,000 in savings from my summer job and little knowledge of the country beyond *Crocodile Dundee*.

It was in Sydney that I experienced two things that changed my life forever: the subculture of backpacking and the foodservice industry.

As I backpacked around Australia, I was impacted by how alive with hope and love backpackers' hostels were. Everywhere I stayed, I was invigorated by fellow travellers who exuded honesty and positive energy. People I met were often politically charged and open to new experiences. It seemed that we were constantly creating dialogue that broke down language and racial barriers - that we shared a common sentiment. For the first time since I was a child, I felt as if I were connected to a grander set of values, a larger picture, if you will.

The second realization came shortly after getting my first job in a foodservice establishment: I was born to serve people quality food and drink. The job requires considerable physical stamina and optimism, which I possess.

I excelled at serving and loved my job. As I perfected my craft, I began noticing how different restaurants and bars not only had different gimmicks, they also had different business models. I found myself thinking more critically about how the bar where I worked could be run. Being youthful, confident, and living on the other side of the world from my home, I somehow came up with the idea that I could run a business properly, making it profitable and enjoyable.

Upon returning from Australia, my mind was spinning from all the new perspectives I encountered. My experiences were helping me forge a worldview.

More precisely, by partaking in a different culture, I felt a sense of connection with the world, and I began to feel comfortable with my place in it. Being away from home, supporting myself and feeling good about what I did gave me the confidence to identify my strong points and move forward in life, knowing I had skills I could build on successfully.

I worked hard in various small businesses in Halifax, achieving respect from managers and owners as I soaked up all the knowledge available to me. Desperate for a small sign that my dreams would someday become a reality, I went to a psychic. Maybe she could see the future, or maybe she just planted the seed for manifest destiny, but she told me she could see me behind a counter and I was helping people. She said I would have a business, but wasn't sure what type.

I practically ran to the library and checked out everything associated with opening a café. I spent my early twenties continually visiting and revisiting the concept, all the while honing my skills as server, knowing it would one day benefit me greatly.

When my lifelong friend, David Eisnor, returned to Halifax from travelling overseas, he told me he wanted to open a backpackers' hostel. The fact that a dear friend had experienced a similar epiphany touched me deeply. I felt everything in my life fall into place. I knew this was what I was meant to do. We wrote a business plan and began the daunting task of figuring out the most important aspect of business: location.

It was in this chaotic time that I also met my love, Caley, and his six-year-old son, Rhett. Caley challenges me every day to be the best that I can be, and his love for people and the world greatly enhanced my capabilities for compassion and understanding. Though David and I were enduring major hurdles to our resolve, becoming a stepmom proved to be the most challenging and incredible experience I have had. In the beginning, it was a struggle to go from a self-absorbed 23-year-old youth to stepmom of a six-year-old boy. I loved my new stepson unconditionally and, with time, both our hearts opened, allowing both Rhett and I to love each other, as family should. I feel proud of the relationship we have, and so lucky to have the opportunity to be a part of his life.

Suddenly, in 2001 a property on Gottingen Street became available. I had lived in Halifax's north end for many years and loved it, but I was well aware of the stigma attached to the neighbourhood. David and I pondered the possibilities and decided to go for it because the price was right, and the building owner and operator, Mrs. Lee, really believed in us. When we encountered trouble getting financing, she agreed to rent the building to us, holding a mortgage price for three years. It was a risky move, but we knew that this was the right building, stigma or not. The financing came through and we became the owners. From the start, I knew the building, which only had two previous owners, was a special place, one where families raised children and realized their dreams.

Thanks to Mrs. Lee's confidence, we began the arduous task of renovating the building and starting our business, Halifax Backpackers. This process was by far the most complete test of my strength I have endured. Sure, as a business owner, I still face huge tests of strength and stamina, but back then I had no concept of how overwhelming entrepreneurship really is. Now I do.

There are a lot of people out there who find the entrepreneurial lifestyle interesting, marvelling at the amount of time, energy and dedication that goes into building a successful business. I believe the most difficult aspect of starting a business, though, is finding something you truly love to do.

Since I was basically inspired to create my own company while in Australia, and then by my friend David, it has been easy for me to summon the verve to do almost anything regardless of the circumstances. Growing up running the business has taught me that anything is possible to fix, change or let go.

As I began developing my business and raising my family, I became impassioned by the sociopolitical currents I saw running through my community. Caley had the amazing idea to open a café in the storefront of the building. Watching the community embrace the café as a hub is incredible. I learned the history of the area and its residents, and the realities of living and working in the same community became apparent to me. I also began to notice the impact a backpackers' hostel can have on a community, as our guests were spending money in the area and engaging locals with their travel experiences.

Some people were even forging long-term, powerful ties. Seeing these friendships blossom is what connects me to the culture of backpacking.

The fact that my livelihood, neighbours and friends were a great part of an area widely regarded as rough, or bad, broke my heart. I felt very safe in the North End, mainly because, for the first time, I felt like I belonged to a community. I wanted to do something that would show everybody the true community that, in my mind, was the North End, so I rallied the other merchants to create the Gottingen Street Sunday Market.

The market attracted thousands of people and generated a lot of positive media coverage. Afterward, many interested people got together and created the North End Community Street Festival, an annual daylong event where a block of Gottingen Street is shut down for festivities.

The street markets inspired local merchants who were somewhat jaded after years of slow business. Many could remember Gottingen's heyday as a booming commercial district. Through the markets, they thought it might be possible to experience an upswing again.

My activities on Gottingen Street have led to my most rewarding experiences. I am most engaged at the moment in making sure the area improves in a way that allows all residents to be positively impacted. For example, I have created a mentorship program at my business for people who have minimal job experience.

We provide long, intensive training, with many chances for feedback and discussion.

I invariably find myself learning as much from the amazing people I am working with as they learn from me.

My success with this effort led me to develop a job shadow program for high school youth to help them make connections with local businesses. In my mind, hiring local is as important a practice as buying local, especially in communities where unemployment is an issue.

In April 2004, after the conception of Halifax Backpackers, I had a life-altering year. While in the hospital awaiting the birth of a son, I received three important phone calls. The first was news that the Business Development Bank of Canada named David and me young entrepreneur of the year. The second revealed that I was the recipient of a community leadership award from the Canadian Youth Business Foundation for my work in my neighbourhood. The third brought news that Alexa McDonough nominated me to participate in the Women's Symposium for Leadership, a mentorship program being held by the Lieutenant Governor and Mount Saint Vincent University.

My beautiful son, Holden, was born on April 17, four weeks early but perfectly healthy. Caley, Rhett and I were excited about the new addition to our family.

One month after Holden was born, I attended the Symposium. It offered 100 women in the beginning of their careers an opportunity to benefit from mentors at the height of their careers.

Matches were made based on region and area of specialty. There was a weekend of events organized to get the diverse group of women interacting, ending with the appointment of the mentors. I met so many incredible women, and felt inspired by the speakers.

Topics ranged from successful careers, to healthy communities, to deciding whether to have children. A very inspiring group leader named Pat Watson particularly impressed me. As luck would have it, she was assigned as my mentor.

Pat is a consultant and facilitator, and her reassurance and thoughtful listening have altered my life. She has helped me clearly define concepts I have been trying to understand for years. Her positive outlook on life and tools for resolving conflict have greatly strengthened my ability to be a friend, employer, mother and activist.

By the time you read this, David and I will have finalized the deal that will make me sole owner of our café, hostel and catering company. It is another risky move, and another first day of the rest of my life.

Rites of passage such as this have given me a sense of great accomplishment, yet it's the memories of David and I doing karaoke or my sons and I snowboarding that have given me the most pleasure. I guess living life is not unlike running a business.

Your success isn't measured so much by your official achievements as by the connections you've made to yourself, your family, your community and your world.

~　~　~

MICHELLE STRUM

Michelle Strum owns the Halifax Backpackers and Alteregos Café and Catering. She has been featured in many magazines such as Time and Chatelaine not only for her awards for small business but also for her strong community development passion and successes. Michelle re-established the Gottingen Street Merchants Association, started a yearly street festival and has been diligently working to unite merchants in the Agricola Hydrostone area with Gottingen Street in order to have a stronger voice for the north end of Halifax.

Michelle was awarded the 2004 young entrepreneur award from the Business Development Bank and a national community leadership award from the Canadian Youth Business Foundation. Michelle is currently engaged in a very exciting volunteer project that offers employment and mentoring to youth in the Uniacke Square area.

I Am Singing My Song

Patricia Ann Watson

I am singing the song that I came here to sing.
I am bringing the earth all the joy I can bring.
I am dancing to music composed from above,
vibrations of harmony, beauty and love.
I am keeping my life in a natural key,
so that I may become what I came here to be.
I think, so I am; as I'm living I find
that my life has a tempo in tune with my mind.
I am feeling those rhythms within and afar,
directing my heartbeat or guiding a star.
I hear the symphony nature plays.
Composed in eternal and infinite ways.
I am chanting the song that accompanies birth
of wonder and joy of existence on earth!
~ Poet Unknown

When I was a young child, I had a reoccurring dream. I was on stage singing, and saw myself in the audience, or in the audience watching my performance. Over the years, I've come to realize the key message in that dream – to be true to myself. In other words, to do what I love, which is to be a singer and to work with people. This is the song that I've come here to sing. This is the key to my success.

It took me a long time to give voice to this song - my song - and to realize that I am the only one who has control over my life and my thinking.

My journey to find my song began in Plainfield, New Jersey, where I was born on September 4, 1944. I was the oldest of seven children - three boys and four girls. My mother was brought up in a Christian family, so I spent many childhood Sundays at Shiloh Baptist Church. More than the foundation for my belief in a higher power, that church is where I first discovered the power of music. It became my passion, and I sang whenever and wherever I could - church choirs, the glee club at school and in various choral groups.

I might have followed my passion and made it a career had I not listened to, and believed, the many people who told me it would never bring me financial security. Instead, I married at the age of 21 and had a beautiful boy, whom we named John Wesley Howard II. This marriage lasted five years. We decided that we weren't true soul mates and separated. John lived with me for the next seven years, and then went to live with his father for a while before returning to me. These were happy times, but difficult ones. I had a son to raise and provide for, and although he brought great joy into my life, something was missing - a sense of self and a sense of purpose.

At the time, I believed I would find myself through the acceptance of others. I had yet to realize it doesn't happen that way.

One other thing was complicating my search for a sense of self.

Throughout my childhood, I came up against a cultural norm that accepted or favoured white people and their stories over black people. So the role models available to and promoted to me often had nothing to do with my own cultural identity or heritage. I was left without confidence in my own worthiness. This empty feeling, coupled with my ongoing search for acceptance and lack of love for myself, led to a long period of drug and alcohol addiction. Drugs and alcohol were a way for me to avoid looking inward. They filled the gap where a sense of self should have been. I stopped looking for myself and caring about who I was.

I was in my early 30s when an incredible opportunity came my way. A photographer, who had been hired by the consulting firm I worked for, asked me if I would be interested in doing a photo shoot and possibly being on an album cover for Houston Pearson, a jazz musician who plays the organ. I went to New York for the photo shoot and the record company accepted the picture. The president of the company found out that I was a singer and offered me the chance to record.

All I had to do was to cut a demo and send it to him. Instead, I backed out, like so many people inexplicably do when they are faced with the possibility of seeing their dreams come true.

I've often thought about what it was that caused me to turn my back on that chance to fulfill my childhood dream. Was I afraid of failure or of success?

Ultimately, I think it was other people's opinions and stories that swayed me. I believed their oft-repeated advice to take the safe road and seek stability instead of following my dream - a career in music. They may have meant well, but by listening to them, I lost the opportunity of a lifetime.

The years that followed brought significant achievements for me. I met and married David, a wonderful, loving man and I completed my college degree. Yet my addictions continued, and there remained a void in my life. Years would pass before I came to the realization I had not and would not become the person I was intended to be if I continued to follow the path I was on.

The "eureka" moment was the realization that I was losing my life, my husband, my family and friends to my addiction. Hard as it would be, I knew I had to shake this monkey off my back to become the person that I was meant to be in this lifetime.

It was time to STOP, but how? The answer came when a friend invited me to attend a service at her spiritual community. I walked in the door and felt right at home, just as I did in my church as a child. It was a profound moment of spiritual awakening, and in it, I found the power to break free from my spiral. I began a renewed search for myself, this time through prayer, meditation, affirmations and using spiritual principles. My transformation had begun. I started by claiming my truth.

What followed was a search and rescue mission of healing.

My goal was to become the person I truly AM - to evolve into my best self. I rid myself of the lie that I was not valuable. I continually affirmed that I have the right to have a beautiful and prosperous life because I was born great. I no longer had to look outside myself to find the treasure; it was already inside me. What I had to do was to accept the qualities that I love about myself and stop feeding myself critical, negative messages as I had done in the past.

Making a change like this was an incredible feat. As I began to open up, to embrace the beautiful person that I am, I noticed wonderful things began to happen. I started to truly notice and appreciate the things I was grateful for, and to understand that my negative thoughts and self-image only attracted more negativity into my life. What's more, I began to own my own power.

No longer would I let anything or anyone define my experience. Whatever my dream, it has been placed within my mind and heart because of the Spirit that is within me. This carries with it everything that is needed to fully and perfectly manifest joy, abundance, love, power and untold treasures. I totally trust in my higher power, which I choose to call God.

Through years of work, study and prayer, I have been reborn as a successful musical artist, inspirational speaker, consultant, facilitator, businesswoman and, above all, a whole person.

Part of this rebirth came when David and I moved to Nova Scotia 10 years ago. For years, David and I had been looking for a place to live when he retired. We looked at areas in the United States and Canada.

We finally found a beautiful spot in East LaHave, Nova Scotia. In this new home, I've followed my heart and forged deep connections with amazing business people and musicians. Amazing things have happened as a result - artistically, spiritually, and professionally.

The consulting business I started before we relocated began to blossom. I became a facilitator of training programs in the Executive and Professional Development program at Saint Mary's University. I also began teaching in the Management Development Program for Women at Mount Saint Vincent University.

I made many contacts and, as a result, my business soared.

Around this time I started taking spiritual classes online and, six years later, I became a licensed Practitioner (Spiritual Counsellor). I now teach spiritual practices online and have started study groups in East LaHave and Haifax, Nova Scotia.

I also began to "sing my own song" this time as a real singer; thus truly finding my voice. Since then, I've led gospel workshops for the Lunenburg Folk Harbour Festival, the United Church in Mahone Bay, Saint Margaret's of Scotland Anglican Church in Halifax and the Harmony Women's Festival in Lockport. I've also sung with the South Shore Women in Jazz. Currently, I am singing jazz with John Bird and John Duckworth, and I continue to perform with the Nova Gospel Ensemble. I've enjoyed some mind-blowing experiences as a singer and am exceptionally grateful for the joy music brings to my soul.

Today, I live my life fully because I am awake and eager to let go of the fear - which Ernest Holms refers to as false evidence appearing real in his textbook *Science of Mind* - that held me back for so many years. I live every moment as the woman I aspire to be. Love, compassion and forgiveness are my guiding principles. Faith in goodness - freely given and received - is my pinnacle for success. The life lessons I take from my experiences are to follow my heart, follow my dreams and everything will unfold as it should. I don't let anything or anyone stand in my way and I continue to be true to myself. That's how I live a fulfilled life. My power exists within me. I know that at the centre of my being is a Divine Person. This source is my real creative power; it is who I am. I venture forth with the will to do, the determination to be and a joy in becoming. I am on the right course (taken out...and moving forward). My secret to success is to set an intention and not let anything interfere in achieving it. At last, I am singing my song for all to hear.

My Affirmation for Living:
I raise my sense of personal value, as I was born under a singing star.
I accept my Divine birthright and revel in the abundance of the universe that constantly fulfills my every claim.
I honour who I am - a spiritual woman of God living in this time and space.
And so it is...Amen!!!

~ ~ ~

PATRICIA ANN WATSON, B.A., RScP

Pat was born in Plainfield, New Jersey and presently lives in East LaHave, Nova Scotia. Her passion and love is singing and Pat sings jazz and gospel music.

She is the President of P.W. Associates, Incorporated which specializes in Management Development and Training. She has over 23 years of experience working with government agencies, gas and oil, pharmaceutical, manufacturing, health care and the hospitality industries – locally, nationally and internationally.

Pat is an adjunct faculty member in the Management Development Program for Women at Mount Saint Vincent University. She also facilitates training programs for Saint Mary's University at the World Trade Centre. She is also the East Coast Program Director for the Schulich School of Business Masters Certficate in Project Management. Pat recently received her license as a Practitioner (RScP – Religious Science Practitioner) in Spiritual Counseling. She is a member of the Canadian Association of Professional Speakers, the Centre for Women in Business and the South Shore Women's Network.

Pat is a graduate of Antioch University and has taken graduate courses towards her master's degree in Organizational Development at American University.

About the Editors

Kaye Parker

Kaye is a facilitator, trainer, coach, author, and president of PBBA Atlantic. She has a background as a teacher (Education, UNB; Adult Education, St. Francis Xavier University), and her accreditation with the Canadian Public Relations Society, her designation from the Canadian Human Resources Association, as well as advanced qualifications to administer and interpret the Myers Briggs Type Inventory. She has trained as a personal efficiency coach, and as a professional recruiter. She is the founder and president of the training and consulting firm of PBBA Atlantic Inc.

Kaye has more than fifteen years of industry experience in management positions at the senior level, both in the government and private sector. In addition, Kaye has been a journalist and a writer. She uses her breadth of experience to design and deliver adult learning materials that are practical and that can be put to work immediately. She is a long-standing facilitator for Saint Mary's University Executive and Professional Development Program, the Nova Scotia Government, and has private sector clients from across Atlantic Canada.

Kaye is past-President of the Halifax Chapter of the Canadian Association of Professional Speakers (CAPS). She is a member of Schooner Toastmasters club, the Human Resource Association of Nova Scotia, and the Nova Scotia branch of the Canadian Public Relations Society.

PAT WATSON, B.A., RSCP.

Pat was born in Plainfield, New Jersey and presently lives in East LaHave, Nova Scotia. Her passion and love is singing and she sings jazz and gospel music. She has just released a new jazz and gospel music CD entitled, "Feeling Good", and has been living her dream across North America.

Pat is the President of P.W. Associates, Incorporated which specializes in Management Development and Training. She has over 25 years of experience working with government agencies, gas and oil, pharmaceutical, manufacturing, health care and the hospitality industries -locally, nationally and internationally.

Pat has been adjunct faculty member in the Management Development Program for Women at Mount Saint Vincent University. She facilitated training programs for Saint Mary's University at the World Trade Centre, and was the East Coast Program Director for the Schulich School of Business Masters Certficate in Project Management.

Pat recently received her license as a Practitioner (RScP in Spiritual Counseling. She is a member of the Canadian Association of

Professional Speakers, the Centre for Women in Business and the South Shore Women's Network.

Pat is a graduate of Antioch University and has taken graduate courses towards her master's degree in Organizational Development at American University.